A Chaste
Maid in
Cheapside

NEW MERMAIDS

General editors:
Brian Gibbons, Professor of English Literature,
University of Münster
William C. Carroll, Boston University
Tiffany Stern, University College, University of Oxford

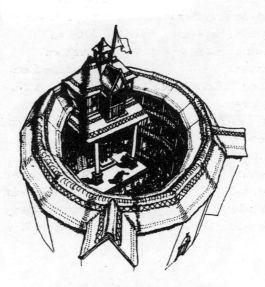

Reconstruction of an Elizabethan Theatre
by C. Walter Hodges

NEW MERMAIDS

'The True Likeness' (*Vera Effigies*) of Thomas Middleton.
An engraving published in November 1795 by W. Richardson.

THOMAS MIDDLETON

A CHASTE MAID IN CHEAPSIDE

edited by Alan Brissenden
Adelaide University

A & C Black • London
WW Norton • New York

Second edition 2002
Reprinted 2006, 2007
A & C Black Publishers Limited
38 Soho Square
London W1D 3HB
www.acblack.com

ISBN 978–0–7136–5068–6

First New Mermaid edition 1968
Ernest Benn Limited

A CIP catalogue record for this book is available from the British Library

This book is produced using paper made from wood grown in managed, sustainable forests. It is natural, renewable and recyclable. The logging and manufacturing processes conform to the environmental regulations of the country of origin.

Printed in Great Britain by Cox and Wyman Ltd, Reading, Berkshire

CONTENTS

ACKNOWLEDGEMENTS

A. H. Bullen's *The Works of Thomas Middleton* (8 vols. 1885–86) is still the standard edition but I have also used those of Dyce (5 vols., 1840) and Ellis (Mermaid Series, 2 vols., 1887–90) as well as R. J. Wall's unpublished dissertation, 'A Critical Edition of Thomas Middleton's *A Chast Mayd in Cheape-side*' (University of Michigan, 1958). *Shakespeare's Bawdy* (1956) by Eric Partridge, *A Topographical Dictionary to the Works of Shakespeare and his Fellow Dramatists* (Manchester, 1925) by E. H. Sugden and M. P. Tilley's *Dictionary of the Proverbs in England in the Sixteenth and Seventeenth Centuries* (Ann Arbor, 1950) have been indispensable reference books.

My sincere thanks are due to Mrs Edith Lack and Mrs Jane Delin, who saved me much tedium in hunting references, to my colleagues at the University of Adelaide, especially F. H. Mares, M. Bryn Davies and G. W. Turner, and to A. M. Gibbs of the University of Leeds. I am also grateful to Miss Pat Story for her typing, Miss Rebecca Foale for her cartography and the General Editors for their patience. To my wife and family I owe a special debt for accepting so nobly and for so long the presence of another woman in the house.

(FIRST EDITION, 1968)

The reprint of 1971 gave opportunity to correct misprints, make corrections and alterations and additions, and to thank Elizabeth Sweeting, the then Administrator of the Oxford Playhouse, for sending details of the 1970 OUDS production of the play.

For the present edition the text has been considered afresh in the light of those which have been published since 1968, and the notes and Introduction have been revised and expanded. I am grateful to the General Editor for helpful suggestions, and to the staff of the Barr Smith Library, Adelaide University, and the Victoria and Albert Theatre Museum, London, for cheerful assistance. For information on the 1997 production at Shakespeare's Globe I thank Nick Robins and others on the theatre staff.

Since the first New Mermaid edition of 1968 *A Chaste Maid in Cheapside* has been edited by Charles Barber for Fountainwell Texts (Edinburgh, 1969), R. B. Parker for the Revels Plays (1969), Kenneth Muir in *Thomas Middleton: Three Plays* (1975), David Frost in *Selected Plays of Thomas Middleton* (Cambridge, 1978) and Bryan Loughrey and Neil Taylor in *Thomas Middleton: Five Plays* (Harmondsworth, 1988). All these editions have been drawn on for this revision and are referred to in the notes by the names of the respective editors. The first collected edition of Middleton's dramatic works since Bullen's, under the general editorship of Gary Taylor, is scheduled for publication by Oxford University Press in 2003.

I am again grateful to my wife and family for their helpful support.

A. B.

ADELAIDE 2002

ABBREVIATIONS

Q	the edition of 1630
Bullen	A. H. Bullen, *The Works of Thomas Middleton* (1885–86)
Dyce	Alexander Dyce, *The Works of Thomas Middleton* (1840)
ed.	editions other than this
N&Q	*Notes and Queries*
PMLA	*Publications of the Modern Language Association of America*
PQ	*Philological Quarterly*
RORD	*Research Opportunities in Renaissance Drama*
SEL	*Studies in English Literature*
s.d.	stage direction
s.p.	speech prefix
Survey	John Stow, *A Survey of London*, ed. C. L. Kingsford (Oxford, 1908)
Wall	R. J. Wall, 'A Critical Edition of Thomas Middleton's *A Chast Mayd in Cheape-side*', unpublished dissertation (Michigan, 1958)

INTRODUCTION

The Place

First mentioned in 1067 as 'Westceape', as 'Chepsyde' in 1510 and deriving its name from 'ceap', the Anglo-Saxon word for barter, the wide street of Cheapside was the old market place of London, extending from the north-east corner of St Paul's churchyard to the Poultry. Down the centre stood four structures: at the western end the Little Conduit by St Paul's gate, then, three storeys high, one of the twelve crosses set up by Edward I to mark the resting-places of Queen Elinor's body on its way from Lincoln to Westminster Abbey after her death in 1290; next was the Standard, a square pillar with a conduit, and a statue of Fame on the top, and at the eastern end, where Cheapside met the junction of Bucklersbury and Poultry, stood the Great Conduit, first built in 1285, to which water was piped from Paddington. The conduits – water reservoirs – ran red wine on special occasions, including the triumphal Progress of James I through London on 15 March 1604, and those with flat tops served as stages for shows during such events. From the fourteenth century to the eighteenth Cheapside provided the culminating point on the main processional route through the city for royal entries to London and major civic observances, particularly the inauguration of the Lord Mayor.[1] Many of the side streets were named after the trade guilds which lived and worked there (bakers in Bread Street, dairymen in Milk Street, fishmongers in Friday Street), and the Mermaid tavern, frequented by Shakespeare, Jonson, Donne and other poets and playwrights, stood in Bread Street. Goldsmiths Row, the part of Cheapside between Bread and Friday streets, and built in the year 1491, was to the historian John Stow 'the most beautiful frame of fair houses and shops that be within the walls of London, or elsewhere in England ... It containeth in number ten fair dwelling-houses and fourteen shops, all in one frame, uniformly built four storeys high ... [the front] was again new painted and gilt over in the year 1594'. Cheapside itself, he said, 'is worthily called, the Beauty of London'.[2] Stow describes grimmer sights when he lists executions which had taken place at the Standard; criminals and prostitutes – *un*chaste maids – were still punished by whipping and carting along the length of the street in

---

[1] See Lawrence Manley, *Literature and Culture in Early Modern London* (Cambridge, 1997), pp. 212–93.

[2] *Survey*, I, 345; John Stow, *Annals of Great Britain* (1615), p. 859.

the seventeenth century, and there was a pillory at the eastern end. In 1912 a hoard of early seventeenth-century jewellery, now in the Museum of London, was dug up, presumably hidden by thieves or by a goldsmith fleeing fire or plague. Cheapside has remained a commercial centre.

The Author

Thomas Middleton was christened at St Lawrence Jewry, not a hundred and fifty metres north of Cheapside, on 18 April 1580. His life spans the greatest period in English drama, for he was buried on 4 July 1627 at St Mary's, Newington Butts, about two kilometres south of Southwark. His father, William, a bricklayer and builder, was a gentleman with his own coat of arms who owned or leased property near the Curtain Theatre in Shoreditch and at Limehouse. Ten months after William died in January 1586 his widow Anne, forty-eight years old, married Thomas Harvey, an impoverished grocer and seaman in his twenties, who had been with Ralegh in the failed Roanoke Island colony. Getting his hands on the Middleton property seems to have been Harvey's principal aim, and this also appears to have been the motive for Allen Waterer's marriage to Avice Middleton, Thomas's sister, in 1596. Harvey fled the country to avoid creditors in 1595 but returned later. Legal squabbles over property continued to disrupt the family throughout Thomas's early years. Even after her first husband's death, Avice and her second husband, John Empson, took up litigation, still over property, against Waterer's brother. Middleton himself married about 1602, as his son Edward was aged nineteen in 1623. His wife Mary was the granddaughter of the composer and organist John Marbeck and her brother was for a time an actor with the Admiral's Men. She was probably the Maulyn Marbeck who was christened on 9 July 1575 at St Dunstan's in the West; this agrees with the name of the playwright's widow, given as Magdalen, who applied in February 1627/28 for a gift of money from the city of London; she was granted twenty nobles, but was probably little more trouble to the aldermen as she died in the following July and was buried at Newington. One can only wonder why Middleton gave a variation of the same name to the sentimental, vulgar, acquisitive goldsmith's wife of his play.

The playwright matriculated in April 1598 at Queen's College, Oxford, the most popular college of the time, and although in 1600 he sold his share of the family property to his brother-in-law Waterer so that he could stay there he had to return to London to help his mother in one of her lawsuits in 1601 and apparently did not graduate. He was then said to have been seen in London 'daily accompanying the players'.[3] By the time he was twenty he had published some verse: *The Wisdom of Solomon Paraphrased* (1597), a tedious and lengthy piece which even an apologist calls 'a stupefying read',[4] *Micro-Cynicon* (1599), an attempt at Marstonian satire, and *The Ghost of Lucrece* (1600), a dull poem in the complaint tradition. By May 1602 he was writing for Philip Henslowe, the entrepreneurial theatre owner, who notes him collaborating with Munday, Drayton, Webster and perhaps others on *Caesar's Fall*, a play now lost, and two years later he published two prose tracts attacking low-life vices. By this time he had almost certainly begun his career as a playwright with *The Family of Love* (c. 1602), a lively satire on sectaries in which he uses the twin themes of sex and wealth for the first time. The fact that his sister Avice's brother-in-law was a Brownist who had been in Newgate for his beliefs (followers of the dissident Robert Browne, the Brownists later became known as Congregationalists) may have significance for Middleton's consistent ridicule of Puritans, but they were fair game for many writers of the time.

Of about fifty dramatic works that have been ascribed to Middleton at some time, thirteen plays have been suggested as his unaided works, the rest being collaborations or masques and entertainments. A growing relationship with the city authorities is suggested by his writing a poetical oration which was delivered before the King, Queen and Prince Henry during the progress through London in 1604, but it was not until 1613 that he wrote the first of a number of pageants and entertainments for the city of London.[5] In 1620 he was appointed City Chronologer to record the memorable acts and occurrences of the city, a post in which he was succeeded by Ben Jonson.

Middleton's published plays fall conveniently, if loosely, into three groups: city comedies, which end triumphantly with *A Chaste Maid in Cheapside* (1611–13), romances like *The Widow* (1616), and the great tragedies, *The Changeling*, with Rowley (1622), and *Women Beware Women* (1621–7). In 1624 he wrote the brilliant occasional satire *A Game at Chess*, which ran for nine days at the Globe and got the King's Men into trouble with their patron.[6]

---

[3] See P. G. Phialas, 'Middleton's Early Contact with the Law', *Studies in Philology*, 51 (1955), 186–94.

[4] G. B. Shand, 'The Elizabethan Aim of *The Wisdom of Solomon Paraphrased*', in K. Friedenreich, '*Accompaninge the Players*': *Essays Celebrating Thomas Middleton, 1580–1980* (New York, 1983), pp. 67–77.

[5] David Bergeron discusses Middleton's use of similar material for very different ends in 'Middleton's Moral Landscape: *A Chaste Maid in Cheapside* and *The Triumphs of Truth*' in Friedenreich, pp. 133–46.

[6] For a discussion of Middleton's relationship with King James see W. Power, 'Thomas Middleton vs. King James I', *N&Q*, 202 (1957), 526–34.

Middleton, as well as the players, was summoned before the Privy Council, but no action seems to have been taken when he failed to appear, and his son Edward was called to answer for him.

His early unaided plays were written for the children's companies of Paul's and Blackfriars; after they disbanded in 1606 he wrote for Prince Henry's (formerly the Admiral's) Men and the Lady Elizabeth's company, but mostly for the King's Men. His early life clearly influenced his writing: his father's house was in Ironmongers Lane, off Cheapside, and he was in every sense a Londoner; at the same time he remembered Oxford with affection and his university fools are all from Cambridge; sex, property-hunger and litigation were closely related in the unfortunate course of his family's affairs after his father's death, and the bitterness and dismay which he probably felt at that time must surely have resulted in attitudes which colour the greater part of his best work.

Date

Internal evidence indicates 1613 rather than earlier as the date of the play's composition. R. C. Bald draws attention to the tightening of laws against killing and eating meat during Lent in 1613, which gives a topical background for the scene with the promoters (II.ii). However the reinforcement of these Lenten acts began in 1608, and was repeated each year, so this evidence is not unassailable. The flattering portrayal of the watermen in Act IV can be seen as support for their agitation against the building of theatres north of the Thames; a falling off of the theatrical trade to the Bankside during 1613 had meant a considerable loss to them, and a petition was sent to King James in January 1614. The main relevant passage (IV.ii.6–12) puts the Blackfriars theatre specifically in a bad light, presenting it as a rowdy and dangerous place. (No evidence has yet been found that the incident described really occurred.)

Another strong indication of 1613 as the most likely date lies in Allwit's boast that when his wife is in childbed 'A lady lies not in like her; there's her embossings, / Embroiderings, spanglings, and I know not what,' (I.ii.32–3) and the christening guest's comment, 'See gossip and she lies not in like a countess' (III.ii.99). These remarks would have had particular relevance soon after the extravagant lying in of the Countess of Salisbury at the end of January 1613 (see note to III.ii.99); and then there is Allwit's calling the baby 'little countess' (II.ii.27). In his Revels edition of the play, R. B. Parker gathers together these and other contemporary events, including the formation in 1611 of the Lady Elizabeth's Men, their amalgamation with the Queen's Revels, a boys' company, and their performing in the Swan Theatre between August of that year and October 1614, to agree with a first performance date between March and August 1613.

Sources

Middleton appears to have invented the stories of the play, though he may have taken ideas from several sources. Elizabeth Buckingham[7] argues persuasively that an epigram in Campion's *Art of English Poesie* (1602) is a direct source for the Allwit-Whorehound plot (see Appendix A); a situation similar to Allwit's is also the subject of a contemporary ballad, 'Who would not be a cuckold', which makes special reference to social climbing in the city (see Appendix A). Shanti Padhi makes a good case for Allwit's being modelled on the eponymous willing husband in the Spanish novel *Guzmán de Alfaranche*, by Mateo Aleman;[8] A. H. Gilbert suggests that Middleton may have used an Italian treatise on marriage;[9] and Dekker's *Bachelor's Banquet* (1603) could have provided him with material for the christening scene. It is just possible that he may have intended personal satire in the character of Yellowhammer, since a suit for debt was brought against Middleton, among others, by Robert Keysar, a goldsmith of Cheapside, in 1609.

The Play

The comedies Middleton wrote for the children's companies, especially *Michaelmas Term, A Mad World, My Masters* and *A Trick to Catch the Old One* (all c. 1606–1607), show a mastery of material and a firm satiric intent, but none attains the marvellous unity of tone and headlong vitality of *A Chaste Maid*. The play was largely neglected by critics until the 1930s – T. S. Eliot does not mention it in his seminal essay on Middleton of 1927, although forty years earlier A. C. Swinburne had acclaimed it as having much 'humour, though very little chastity' and engagingly described it as 'a play of quite exceptional freedom and audacity, and certainly one of the drollest and liveliest that ever broke the bounds of propriety or shook the sides of merriment'. L. C. Knights in 1938 and Margot Heinemann in 1980 included the play in their explorations of Middleton as a social commentator. More recent studies have considered Middleton's final success in combining a wide range of atti-

[7] E. L. Buckingham, 'Campion's *Art of English Poesie* and Middleton's *Chaste Maid in Cheapside*', *PMLA*, 43 (1928), 784–91.

[8] Shanti Padhi, 'Middleton's Wittol in *A Chaste Maid*, and *Guzmán de Alfaranche*', *N&Q*, n.s. 31 (1984), 234–6.

[9] A. H. Gilbert, 'The Prosperous Wittol in Giovanni Battista Modio and Thomas Middleton', *Studies in Philology*, 41 (1944), 235–7.

tudes, his moral and critical analysis of city society, the coexistence of the delicious and the disgusting in the play, the symbolism of fluids representing male potency and female weakness, and the relationship between the carnal and the religious. In the only book exclusively devoted to Middleton's city comedies, Anthony Covatta considers that the 'play constitutes a crowded yet spacious celebration of life', and in a closely detailed discussion, Swapan Chakravorty argues that 'Sexual negotiations map out the division of power between gentry and citizenry [a division which] highlights collusion rather than conflict'.[10] There is universal agreement that *A Chaste Maid* is Middleton's finest comedy. He welds into a complex whole the themes of corruption, money and sex which are particularly his so that we laugh, often uproariously, even while we are chilled with faint horror and sickened with disgust. In its attitudes to vice and punishment *A Chaste Maid* looks forward to the later plays, especially *Women Beware Women*, in many ways its equivalent in tragedy.

Ironic Designs

All the main characters are corrupt to some degree, even the lovers, Moll Yellowhammer and Touchwood Junior, having to deceive so that they can marry. The tentacles of corruption stretch back into the past and forward into the future: Moll's mother was 'lightsome, and quick' two years before she was married (I.i.9); her father has kept a whore 'and had a bastard, / By Mistress Anne' (IV.i.273–4); Lady Kix, charged with barrenness, indignantly cries, 'I barren! / 'Twas otherways with me when I was at court' (III.iii.54–5); and her sister has had twins, seven months after marriage (II.i.171ff.). Even minor figures like the Country Wench and the Parson are ripely corrupt – she claims at first that she was a virgin before meeting Touchwood Senior (II.i.70) but later says that her present child is her fifth (II.i.104); the Parson says he has 'felt the force of love'

---

[10] See T. S. Eliot, 'Thomas Middleton', *Selected Essays* (1951), pp. 161–70; A. C. Swinburne, 'Thomas Middleton', *Thomas Middleton*, ed. H. Ellis, I (1887), xviii–xix; L. C. Knights, *Drama and Society in the Age of Jonson* (1937); Margot Heinemann, *Puritanism and Theatre: Thomas Middleton and Opposition Drama Under the Early Stuarts* (Cambridge, 1980); Alexander Leggatt, *Citizen Comedy in the Age of Shakespeare* (Toronto, 1973), pp. 138–43; Brian Gibbons, *Jacobean City Comedy*, 2nd edn (1980), pp. 127–30; S. Wigler, 'Thomas Middleton's *A Chaste Maid in Cheapside*: The Delicious and the Disgusting', *American Imago*, 33 (1976), 197–215; Gail Kern Paster, 'Leaky Vessels: The Incontinent Women of City Comedy', *Renaissance Drama*, 18 (1987), 43–65; Anthony Covatta, *Thomas Middleton's City Comedies* (Lewisburg, 1973), p. 161; Swapan Chakravorty, *Society and Politics in the Plays of Thomas Middleton* (Oxford, 1996), p. 105.

from young women (III.i.3). The action of the play moves in an ambience of illicit sex, which will continue in the future as Touchwood Senior becomes a professional adulterer (V.iv.83) and the Allwits decide to set up a brothel in the Strand (V.i.170).

All the sexual relationships except the young lovers' are directed by greed (or need) for money, and this greed overrides all else, especially affecting family loyalties.[11] Allwit, the complaisant (and complacent) cuckold, and his wife live off Sir Walter Whorehound, Mistress Allwit's lover and father of her seven children; Davy, Sir Walter's kinsman, hopes the wealthy knight will die so that he can gain an inheritance. The Allwits are a commercial enterprise rather than a married couple bound by mutual love; they have little or no feeling, either for each other or anyone else. There is perhaps more human feeling between Maudline Yellowhammer and her husband, but they have little for their children except in so far as they are business assets – Tim, the Cambridge boy, because he is rising socially in the world and going to marry a Welsh heiress, Moll because she is the bait to land a rich knight, even though he may be diseased. In each case the marriage will bring to the tradesman that socially necessary commodity, land. Their attitudes are shaped almost exclusively by their lust for lucre. When she thinks Moll is dying, Maudline tries to revive her by saying, 'Look but once up, thou shalt have all the wishes of thy heart / That wealth can purchase' (V.ii.94–5), and when she is thought dead, their fading hopes of riches revive with the thought that Tim is going to marry – 'We'll not lose all at once, somewhat we'll catch' (V.ii.115). Her cruelty to Moll is due also to the frustration of Maudline's social ambitions, for the Yellowhammers are more socially conscious than any of the other characters. The goldsmith stresses that Moll, being his daughter, is 'no gentlewoman' (I.i.188), and that when Tim proceeds to his degree he will be 'Sir Yellowhammer then / Over all Cambridge, and that's half a knight' (I.i.154–5). When they think Moll gone, Yellowhammer's concern is that 'All the whole street will hate us' (V.ii.107). In the other two families in the play, wealth and sex are the means of uniting bonds rather than destroying them. Touchwood Senior and his wife, who have had to part because they have too many children and can afford no more, are invited to live at the expense of Sir Oliver Kix, whose own marriage is retrieved when Touchwood Senior impregnates Lady Kix, Sir Oliver believing, of course, that he himself is the prospective father. These two families are treated by the playwright with less seriousness, less bitterness than the Allwits and Yellowhammers. No shudder lies

---

[11] See Samuel Schoenbaum, 'A Chaste Maid in Cheapside and Middleton's City Comedy', in Studies in the English Renaissance Drama, ed. Josephine W. Bennett et al. (New York, 1959), pp. 287–309.

behind the laughter aroused by the Touchwoods and Kixes. This is partly because Kix is a cheerful old fool, and there is genuine affection between him and his wife, and real love between the Touchwoods; there is none between the Allwits and little between the Yellowhammers.

In an elaborate analysis of the plots in A Chaste Maid Richard Levin[12] argues that the families balance each other and that the two married couples and their attendant cuckolds are in symmetrical opposition. Levin distinguishes four plots. In the first, which derives from Roman New Comedy, the young lovers Touchwood Junior and Moll Yellowhammer eventually defeat the opposition of Moll's mercenary, unsympathetic parents and achieve marriage; this romance is comically opposed by the least developed action, the farcical antiromance of Tim Yellowhammer's marrying a whore. The second plot, concerning Sir Walter Whorehound's relationship with his fecund mistress, Mrs Allwit, and her self-satisfied cuckold of a husband, is inversely matched by the third, in which the barrenness of Sir Oliver and Lady Kix's marriage is cured by the fertility of Touchwood Senior. Sir Walter provides the link between these four plots. Foiled in his attempt to marry Moll, he succeeds in marrying off his whore, the Welsh Gentlewoman, but he is turned out of the Allwits' house when they discover he is not only wounded and likely to die, but that even if he survives Lady Kix's child will disinherit him, leaving him destitute. There are, however, other contrasts which Levin's scheme, brilliant as it is, does not have room to include. The Yellowhammers and the Kixes are opposed, for instance, in the way the first want to be rid of their children and the second want to get children; they are linked in their common reason – greed for land and money. A Kix child will gain Sir Walter's wealth for its parents, and the marriages of Moll and Tim will enrich theirs, or so they believe. Ruby Chatterji takes issue with Levin on the grounds that he over-emphasizes plot relationships, arguing that the family is the functional unit which becomes the focus of the play and suggesting that Sir Walter alone among the characters is punished because 'he undermines the very concept of marriage in a citizen household, and also seeks to thrive on the barrenness of another couple'.[13] The super-potent Touchwood Senior does this, however, and he is rewarded. The salient point is that Sir Walter, the play's pivotal character, and the only one who changes morally, is punished physically: when this happens the scales fall from his eyes and he sees the ordinary world. He can no longer stay

[12] R. Levin, The Multiple Plot in English Renaissance Drama (Chicago, 1971), pp. 194–202.
[13] R. Chatterji, 'Theme, Imagery and Unity in A Chaste Maid in Cheapside', Renaissance Drama, 8 (1965), 105–26.

in the callous, inhuman society of the Allwits and Yellowhammers, and fundamentally he is better off; but the necessary price for salvation is physical mortification. From his first appearance Sir Walter is given humane qualities, having a care for his Welsh mistress, being distressed and angry at the Yellowhammer's cruelty to Moll, and having intimations of mortality when he is wounded by Touchwood Junior. He at least has a spiritual victory of sorts. The other characters are punished too, but their punishment lies in their spiritual desiccation. Hippolito, in *Women Beware Women*, speaks of man coming by destruction, 'which oft-times / He wears in his own bosom' (II.i.3–4),[14] and this is true of most of the characters in *A Chaste Maid*.

The knight has his revelation, the others do not, and the theme of blindness, developed so fully in the great tragedies, is quietly present in *A Chaste Maid*. For Sir Walter, his misbegotten children stand between him and the 'sight of Heaven' (V.i.72), for instance. The main use of the theme, however, is characteristically ironic – the Welsh Gentlewoman's mountains are so high 'you cannot see the top of 'em' (I.i.136); the motto inside Touchwood Junior's ring for Moll is, 'Love that's wise, blinds parents' eyes' (I.i.199); Yellowhammer probably wears glasses, but is so blind to what is going on that he is wryly advised to 'put on a pair more' (III.i.26–7); and the foolish Tim, bewailing his marriage to a whore, says, 'I was promised mountains, / But there's such a mist, I can see none of 'em' (V.iv.99–100).

Irony informs the whole structure of the play and contributes to its remarkable unity.[15] The relationship of the Allwits and the Kixes provides a fine example of irony in the plot. Allwit, who lives off the proceeds of his cuckoldom by Sir Walter Whorehound, is set against Sir Oliver, who pays Touchwood Senior for making him a cuckold. Sir Walter descends from riches to poverty, believes he has taken a life and is turned from the house he maintains; Touchwood rises to wealth by creating life and is invited to make his home with the ignorant victim and his family. Sir Walter repents of his sin, Touchwood looks forward to a prosperous sinful future. The plots are linked, again ironically, by Touchwood Junior, who deprives Sir Walter of his bride, Moll, and, by encouraging his brother's adventure with the Kixes, disinherits him as well. The audience can hardly draw a moral from Sir Walter's repentance, as it is counterbalanced

---

[14] Unless otherwise stated, references to Middleton's works apart from *A Chaste Maid* are to the eight-volume edition by A. H. Bullen (1885–86).

[15] As well as those already mentioned, writers who comment on this aspect of the play include U. M. Ellis-Fermor, *The Jacobean Drama* (1961), pp. 135–8, and R. B. Parker, 'Middleton's Experiments with Comedy and Judgement', in *Jacobean Theatre*, ed. J. R. Brown and B. Harris (1960), pp. 179–99.

by Touchwood's cheerful acceptance of the lucrative role of adulterer. Middleton, unlike John Marston, is detached enough to let the points make themselves, one situation the inversion of the other.

Language

Always reinforcing the irony of plot and action is Middleton's use of words. The title of the play itself is ironic, since Cheapside maids were not noted for their chastity. Thomas Dekker writes that 'A fair wench is to be seen every morning in some shop in Cheapside: And in summer afternoons the self-same fair opens her booth at one of the garden-houses about Bunhill'.[16] Garden-houses were notorious places for assignations. The language often gains ironic force from its context, as in the case of the posy for Moll's wedding ring (I.i.199). Sometimes irony is due to the character who is saying the words, for example the Puritans in Act III, who can scarcely speak without producing double meanings. Subtlety and depth can come in single phrases, as when Allwit says he shall be 'hare-mad' (III.ii.214); hares grow wild in the breeding season, around March, the time of the play's action, but even though his wife is breeding, Allwit is not the cause. A single word can illuminate character and situation and condense several implications; 'green goose' (II.ii.83), for instance, is both a young goose, ready for making into goose pie, and a simpleton, but also a cuckold; 'smelt' and 'gudgeons' (IV.ii.51, 53) both imply foolishness and contribute to the aura of stupidity which surrounds Tim Yellowhammer.

Clues to the characters' attitudes to one another are given by the use of personal pronouns. As E. A. Abbott showed long ago in *A Shakespearian Grammar* (1873), emotions, social standing and relationships could be indicated by how 'you' and forms of 'thou' were used, although such usages were not strict or inflexible. Yellowhammer, for instance, uses 'thou' to the carrier from Cambridge, who is socially inferior, but he and Maudline use familial 'you' to Moll until venting their anger on her, when she gets 'thou'. Allwit 'thou's Sir Walter consistently, as an obsequious inferior to a superior, until the wounded knight is no further use to him, when he changes to a contemptuous 'you'. Touchwood Junior and Moll use the affectionate 'thou' to each other all the time.

If modern audiences cannot be expected to recognize such long-lost subtleties as these, they are soon made aware of the technique of *double entendre* – double meaning; Maudline's reminiscences

---

[16] Thomas Dekker, *The Owl's Almanac* (1618), p. 8. For evidence that whores frequented the vicinity of Bunhill see E. H. Sugden, *A Topographical Dictionary to the Works of Shakespeare and his Fellow Dramatists* (Manchester, 1925), pp. 83–4.

about her 'dancing master' (I.i.14–17) are sexual, as are such phrases as Allwit's reference to the knight's supporting him and his wife 'with a prop' (III.ii.75) and Sir Oliver Kix's firm assertion 'Nay I'm not given to standing' (III.iii.136). There is a good deal of more obvious punning, especially in the slapstick scenes with Tim and the Welsh Gentlewoman, and Middleton has fun with broken Latin, in one case fashioning nearly a page of dialogue on one Latin phrase (IV.i.59–80). He adds to the play's sexual charge by exploiting the meaning of 'wit' as sexual organ as well as cleverness; ironically in the name 'Allwit', and elsewhere as commented on in the notes.[17] It is to this kind of bawdiness that Swinburne was referring when he remarked on the play's 'quite exceptional freedom', in other words, sexual allusiveness. The first line makes play with the words 'virginals' and before a dozen lines are out, dancing is mentioned, the first of the many euphemisms for sexual intercourse that occur throughout the play. They end only with Tim's declaration that he will love the whore he's married 'for her wit, I'll pick out my runts there' (V.iv.121–2), that is he'll love her for her sexual organ and dig there for his offspring. The words 'cunt' and 'fuck' are not used by Middleton any more than they were by his fellow dramatists, but like them he uses them in puns, and he alludes to them both in many different ways, as he also does to 'penis'. (These words are used at times in the notes to this edition for conciseness in explanation.) There is good reason to believe that the prurient attitude towards sexual activity and bodily functions which reached its height in the Victorian period did not develop until the later seventeenth century – a famous manifestation of this historical development being the *Family Shakespeare* edited by Henrietta Bowdler and her brother Thomas and published in 1818, in which, according to the title page, 'those words and expressions are omitted which cannot with propriety be read aloud in a family'. There can be no doubt, however, that the audience of Shakespeare and Jonson and Middleton would have laughed at the double and triple layers of meaning in the dialogue of *A Chaste Maid*, and admired the wit (in the sense of cleverness) of the ingenious playwright. More liberal attitudes in the second half of the twentieth century led to the recovery of meanings and so to a richer understanding of both the attitudes and the achievements of Elizabethan and Jacobean dramatists. Lexicographers and scholars such as Eric Partridge, E. A. M. Colman, Frankie Rubinstein and Gordon Williams opened the windows and doors which had been closed for over three hundred years, and audiences at the new Globe on Bankside have laughed with gusto at the play's sexual jesting.

Wordplay is an essential part of the imagery which is also import-

---

[17] See Shakespeare, *As You Like It*, ed. Alan Brissenden (Oxford, 1993), pp. 229–31.

ant for the play's unity. Middleton's use of images of food and animals, for instance, which emphasizes the themes of greed and car-
nality, can be compared with Jonson's in *Volpone* and Webster's in
his two tragedies. The Duchess of Malfi asks her murderers to tell
her brothers that they may 'feed in quiet' when she is dead; the
heavily pregnant Mistress Allwit is 'as great as she can wallow'
(I.ii.6) and 'even upon the point of grunting' (I.ii.31). The theme of
double-dealing which occurs in all the plots is supported by gaming
images; Touchwood Senior 'ne'er played yet / Under a bastard'
(II.i.55–6), Allwit's 'but one peep above a servingman' (I.ii.68–9),
Sir Walter and Touchwood Junior talk in gambling terms as they
duel, and when he hears his wife is pregnant Sir Oliver gleefully
cries he has 'struck it home' as if he's won at tennis (V.iii.19).
Connected with this gaming imagery are the many commercial
images in the play, like Tim's remark that 'Gold into white money
was never so changed' as his half-drowned sister's complexion
(V.ii.20). Such image patterns are markedly similar to those found
in *Women Beware Women*, and reach their most developed form in
A Game at Chess.

The imagery illuminates the corrupt world of Cheapside, and at
the same time enlarges the application of Middleton's moral criticism beyond it. Animals feed off one another, foul one another's
nests, and will, for the most part, go on doing so. His attack on vice
ranges widely, from small follies like the Puritans' dislike of red
hair, because it was Judas's colour, to the Puritans themselves; from
belief in quack medicines, 'waters', to the grand heartlessness and
cupidity of the Allwits and Yellowhammers of the world.
Middleton's satire is harsh, and the play is not lighthearted, as
Richard Barker claims it is. But neither does he begin to lose control, as L. C. Knights suggests.[18] He is, indeed, never more firmly in
control of his material.

The dialogue and the verse contribute much to the pace of the
play. Colloquial abbreviations are constantly used ('is't' for 'is it',
'ha't' for 'have it', for instance) and there are several passages of
dialogue in short, chopped up lines which promote an air of
urgency. By the time Middleton wrote *A Chaste Maid in Cheapside*
his verse had become a highly refined instrument, sensitive to its
context and its content.[19] The smug complacency of Allwit, for

---

[18] Barker, p. 86; Knights, p. 224.
[19] Commenting on the maturity of the verse in another play, *Hengist, King of Kent*
(1616–1620), R. C. Bald remarked that 'the change from the earlier to the later
style is first observable in *A Chaste Maid in Cheapside*, which comes at the very
end of his early comic period' (Middleton, *Hengist King of Kent*, ed. R. C. Bald
(New York, 1938), p. xv).

instance, is reflected rhythmically in his soliloquy, so that he sounds like a grocer checking off the items on a big order.

> I walk out in a morning, come to breakfast,
> Find excellent cheer, a good fire in winter,
> Look in my coal house about midsummer eve,
> That's full, five or six chaldron, new laid up;
> Look in my back yard, I shall find a steeple
> Made up with Kentish faggots, which o'erlooks
> The waterhouse and the windmills; I say nothing
> But smile, and pin the door. When she lies in,
> As now she's even upon the point of grunting,
> A lady lies not in like her ...   (I.ii.23–32)

The change in rhythm in the last lines here points up a transition from outdoors, where there are natural elements, wind and water (and we may note the ironic compression of phallic and religious elements in the word 'steeple'), to the unnaturalness indoors, where a husband acts the pander and the wife, animal-like, is 'upon the point of grunting'.

A broader, more discursive rhythm is used for a scene like the separation of Touchwood and his wife (II.i.1–42) and the balanced metre allows for an occasionally epigrammatic tone, as in

> Some only can get riches and no children,
> We only can get children and no riches   (II.i.11–12)

The most striking use of Middleton's more flowing style is found in the scene of Whorehound's repentance and rejection (V.i). He uses rhyme sparingly, most often to conclude a scene, but also occasionally within a scene to heighten the emotion, as when Moll and Touchwood Junior are about to be married (III.i).

Nineteenth-century editions of the play give a misleading idea of the verse, regularizing metre, modernizing punctuation and smoothing out sentence structure. Parker makes similar changes in his Revels edition. However such rearrangements and additions change the impact of the verse on the reader and, since it is this impact which affects the way the actors will speak and interpret the lines, such alterations ultimately affect the characters and their situations. The irregular verse in fact indicates Middleton's confidence and the flexibility of his medium.

Comic-Satiric

When Jonathan Swift in 1729 wrote *A Modest Proposal for Preventing the Children of poor People in Ireland, from being a Burden to their Parents or Country; and for making them beneficial*

Rory Edwards and Elizabeth Meadows Rouse as Sir Walter Whorehound and Mrs Alwitt in the Globe Theatre's opening season, 1997. Director, Malcolm McKay. Photo, John Tramper.

to the Publick, his benign title concealed the devastatingly ironic proposition that the children be sold as food for the rich. Middleton similarly reverses normal values so convincingly that the audience accepts the world of Cheapside as the real world. Topsy-turveydom reaches its satiric apogee in the Allwit-Whorehound relationship, where the cuckolder takes over so completely that he can jealously accuse the husband of daring to sleep with his own wife and the husband protest that he has not. The comic climax of the play is provided by the reversal of a funeral into a marriage. This world of inverted values and relationships had been arrived at by George Chapman in *The Widow's Tears* (c. 1605) – itself based on the classic fable of the 'widow' of Ephesus – where a husband cuckolds himself to prove his wife's constancy (she claiming later that she knew who it was all the time), and a pronouncement is made that 'It shall be the only note of love to the husband to love the wife: and none shall be more kindly welcome to him than he that cuckolds him' (V.i.306–8). It is exactly this position which Middleton uses to criticise society in *A Chaste Maid*. Where Chapman's play is a development of the action to that point, however, Middleton uses the situation as the continuing condition – Sir Walter's association with the Allwits may end, but Touchwood Senior takes on the same kind of vocation with the Kixes.

The attitude is serious, but the realization is comic. Sir Walter, even in repentance, is overdrawn so that there is a certain amount of undercutting (though the scene can be played so that the character gains audience sympathy). Similarly, the moment of Moll's apparent death emphasizes by contrast the callousness of her parents. We may laugh at Maudline's sentimental 'O, I could die with music' (V.ii.49) as Moll sings her last strain, but the laughter has an undercurrent of disgust. Here Middleton is again using an ironic technique to make his point. (In the Royal Court's 1966 production Moll's song created a moment of genuine pathos, making the comedy all the blacker; quite unexpected, this effect was, as the director William Gaskill said, one of those things that 'just happen' in the theatre.)

The balance of the plots, the consistency of the themes and attitudes, irony, its attendant word usage and imagery all help the play's coherence. Two other related aspects of Middleton's technique are the pace of the action and the localization in time and place. There is no pause in the play's movement; even the two big soliloquies, those of Allwit (I.ii.12–57) and Touchwood Senior (II.i.43–63), extend the action into the past and the future. The scenes are arranged so that the action flows in counterpoint. At the end of Act I, for instance, the Allwit-Whorehound *ménage* makes ready for its seventh birth with all the family present for the occasion. Act II begins with the too-fecund Touchwoods parting because they cannot afford more children. Similar juxtapositions throughout the play make for a tension which helps keep alive the interest of the audience.

By placing the action in Lent, the forty days of fasting before the celebration of Easter, Middleton gives his play a particular focus, sharpening the satire on lust and sensuality. Touchwood Junior works to avoid having to 'pick a famine' (I.i.142), as Christ did in the wilderness, and he and Moll 'die' then are 'resurrected'; the religious significance of the time accentuates Cheapside's mockery of true spiritual values, which are travestied by the christening, where a whoremaster stands godfather to his own bastard, Puritans get drunk and a cuckold beamingly takes the credit for a child not his own. The Country Wench's ruse to get rid of her bastard recalls the play of Mak the shepherd in the medieval Towneley Cycle, and the pervasive air of gluttony and greed is heightened by the contrast given by the season. And Middleton and his audience would have been well aware that Cheapside lay between two meat markets, St Nicholas Shambles off the western end and the Stocks Market at the junction of Poultry and Cornhill.

Detailed localization is a chief characteristic of the play. 'We are eavesdropping on Elizabethan London – the real thing, and not some Italianate mock-up' was the comment of a reviewer who saw a revival of the play in 1956.[20] Middleton was a true Londoner and the city becomes not merely a setting for his characters but a character itself in the action. The streets, the wharves, the taverns, the stairs are all real and necessary. This precision gives a definition and clarity to the action; it provides as well a firm framework to contain outrageously grotesque figures like Maudline Yellowhammer and the monstrous Allwit. One of Middleton's richest achievements is to persuade his audience to accept the inflated perversity of his characters and their situations; his success is at least partly due to the strict accuracy of the scene. While irony may be the most powerful internal force binding the play together, the physical setting is the strongest external means of unity.

The reality of the setting gives greater credibility to the characters and their actions, allowing the audience, especially (one imagines) the contemporary audience, to relate to them, and Middleton's flexible technique encompasses equally the individual close-up, as in Allwit's Act I, scene ii soliloquy, and the wide-screen panorama of the christening and later wedding scenes of III.ii, and V.iv. The play's irony is often reinforced by characters' asides which become direct addresses to the audience, implicating them in the plotting and joking. Although many modern directors feel it necessary to cut the text, add to it, and, especially, bolster the humour with stage business, little of this is truly necessary if the play is presented with

[20] N. S., 'A Chaste Maid in Cheapside', *Manchester Guardian*, 29 November 1956.

speed and clarity. The danger with too much onstage activity is that the verbal humour can be swamped and the moral point being made lost.

The Play on the Stage

A *Chaste Maid* is the only extant play certainly known to have been presented at the Swan Theatre, which, by happy chance, is the subject of the only contemporary drawing of an Elizabethan playhouse interior so far discovered. As this is a fairly crude sketch copied by the Dutch Aernout (or Arend) van Buchell from a drawing by his friend Johannes de Witt, who had visited the theatre in about 1596, its accuracy is questionable, and debate continues about the evidence it provides, though, as R. A. Foakes says, there is nothing in the play which is inconsistent with what the sketch shows.[21] Two doors are called for at V.iv, and '*there is a sad song in the music room*'. The drawing has two doors, but there's no knowing if the gallery with the people in it is the 'music room', or if that is on the next level, hidden in the sketch by the stage canopy. The opening stage direction, with '*a shop being discovered*', is similarly indeterminate: the sketch has no indication of a curtain suspended from an overhang provided by the floor of the first gallery (which could have been drawn aside to 'discover' a shop or stall), much less an inner 'discovery space'. Other plays of the period requiring shops include Thomas Dekker's *The Shoemakers' Holiday* (1599) and Thomas Heywood's *2 If You Know Not Me, You Know Nobody* (1605), and various suggestions have been made as to their staging. Most plausibly, a shop could have consisted of a pair of horizontally-hinged shutters, either in front of the tiring house façade between the doors or in a free-standing structure; when opened, the upper shutter formed a rigid awning and the lower a counter. This arrangement, which was typical of Elizabethan shop windows, is still in use in fairgrounds, street-markets and mobile shops in the western world. As Parker points out, however, the stage directions need not have any relation to the Swan Theatre, or the de Witt-van Buchell drawing.

Although the title page claims that it 'hath beene often acted at the Swan on the Banke-side', there appear to be no contemporary allusions to the play, nor any record of any kind of performance until 16 September 1912, when Patrick Curwen directed an adaptation called *A Posy on the Ring*, cutting the Allwit plot and the Lenten episodes, and performed in a model of the Globe Theatre at

---

[21] See R. A. Foakes, *Illustrations of the English Stage 1580–1642* (1985), pp. xiv–xv, 52–5.

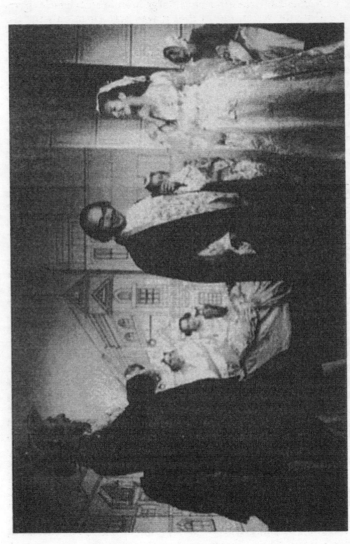

David Tune as the Tutor, Paul Rubens as Tim, and Valerie Mildred as Maudline Yellowhammer. Act III, scene ii in the Adelaide Theatre Group's 1971 production. Director, Alan Brissenden. Photo, Courtesy Valerie Mildred.

the 'Shakespeare's England' exhibition in London. Possibly the special circumstances of the amalgamation of an adult company, the Lady Elizabeth's Men, and the Queen's Revels, a company of boys who could fill the unusually large number of female parts demanded by the script, meant that it was performed only for the one season when it was first written. Indeed it is to be wondered if it was these special circumstances that led to Middleton's writing the play in the way that he did.

Theodore Spencer, S. E. Whicher and John Finch directed a male cast in the play at Harvard University (Eliot House) in December 1953, the first of several university and college productions, mainly in Britain and America. Frederick May produced the first full version recorded in modern England for a season beginning on 26 November 1956 with the Leeds University Union Theatre Group. May used modern dress, with jazz, rock and roll, blues songs and sweaters and jeans. It did not succeed for the critic of the *Manchester Guardian*, who concluded, 'All the same, it whets the appetite. Now let us see the "Chaste Maid" in her true colours.' More kindly, the *Yorkshire Post* thought it 'unusual, imaginative and intriguing' and thought it better to have the young players 'succeed in their natural environment than ... fail in the semblance of a Jacobean costume charade.'

By 2000 more than two dozen productions had been mounted, including Oxford University Dramatic Society's in 1970, directed by the Royal Shakespeare Company's Clifford Williams, which the *Oxford Times* found poorly acted but well produced, and another for the Adelaide Theatre Group, directed by Alan Brissenden, which opened on 10 June 1971. The second of these, which was the play's first Australian production, was presented uncut, on an open stage, in eighteenth-century dress. Critical opinion found it 'quite properly bawdy and enormously entertaining' (*Advertiser*), and a reminder that 'preoccupation with sex is a characteristic not peculiar to the theatre today' (*Sunday Mail*). A one-page glossary was issued with the programme.

In America, David Richman directed a production which 'played to large audiences and received good reviews'[22] with the Upstate Repertory Summer Theater at the University of Rochester in July 1978. In an effort to make the text more intelligible to a modern audience, Richman gave the play a Regency setting, cut several passages, changed Davy Dahumma into Dulcie, conflated several minor characters to enlarge Mrs Touchwood's role and expanded the part of the Welsh Gentlewoman.

William Gaskill directed the first modern professional revival at London's Royal Court Theatre as part of a repertory season which

---

[22] David Richman, 'Directing Middleton's Comedy' in Friedenreich, p. 79.

began on 13 January 1966. The play was adapted by Edward Bond, whose play *Saved* (in which, by contrast, a baby is stoned to death by some bored youths) was also in the season. The costumes, flexibly modern, included Edwardian and contemporary dress. Critical opinion ranged from the growling of the *Evening Standard*, 'five plots – and it's still a bore' (a minority view) to the good sense of *The Times*, 'We could do with a modern Middleton', and the enthusiastic approval of the *Daily Express*, 'Rich in incident, and taken at a brisk, comic-strip pace, this production by the English stage company is witty, wise, and funny, and nobody should miss it.'

The Cherub Company used a virtually uncut text for a significant production which opened at London's Theatre Space on 9 February 1981 with a cast of ten. The doubling necessary made for what R. V. Holdsworth in his review called 'some revealing equations: Touchwood Junior, the play's romantic hero, and Tim, the idiotic Cambridge student, are played by the same person, as are the priapic Touchwood Senior and Tim's Tutor, Lady Kix and the Welsh "niece", and Mistress Yellowhammer and Touchwood Senior's cast-off whore' (*Times Literary Supplement*, 20 March). Calling it 'a marvellous production', Holdsworth said Cherub presented Middleton's great comedy 'as a savage, helter-skelter farce, and its characters as clockwork monsters propelled by lust – for cash, rank and, above all, flesh, human and animal.' He noted, however, that director Andrew Visnevski's 'attempts to ignore or guy' the play's overt moralizing did not work, leaving 'the hard, cynical surface of the comedy untroubled by any didactic earnestness, which is not Middleton's intention.' The production moved to the Upstream Theatre Club, Waterloo, and went on a national tour, followed by performances at the Internationales Festival Kleiner Bühnen in Bern, Switzerland, and at the Buxton International Festival and the Georgian Theatre, Richmond, Yorkshire.

After an absence of some three hundred and eighty-four years, in August 1997 *A Chaste Maid* returned to the Bankside as part of the new Globe Theatre's opening season. The dressing was Jacobean, but the director, Malcolm McKay, who revised the text, used the theatre in a thoroughly modern way. Placards prohibiting the eating of meat during Lent were being put up as the audience arrived, later the audience was encouraged to participate by booing, hissing and cheering, the swordfight went off the stage and down among the groundlings, and Moll's escape was by rope ladder up into the galleries. Sir Walter Whorehound wore an exaggerated pointed wig like a unicorn's horn, emphasizing his phallic potency. For Charles Spencer in the *Daily Telegraph*, the style of playing was 'too broad, encouraging a panto-like response from the audience' but, with a comment on the Globe itself, concluded 'The richly detailed, deceptively low-key acting of Mark Rylance, as a smug husband who calmly prostitutes his wife, suggests that this theatre can happily

Vicky Ogden as Lady Kix and Anthony Best as (a surprisingly young) Sir Oliver Kix in the Cherub Company production, 1981. Director, Andrew Visnevski. Photo, Christopher Pearce.

accommodate artful restraint as well as broader dramatic styles' (29 August). The local setting, the topicality of the themes, the bawdy and the rich array of characters had audiences and most critics applauding.

'Under Malcolm McKay's direction', wrote John Mullan in the *Times Literary Supplement*, 'this comedy, which appears so in need of explanatory annotation in critical editions, comes triumphantly to life ... and the Globe allows for a special gusto in performance' (5 September). The *Observer*'s Kate Kellaway thought the Globe's artistic director, Mark Rylance, 'an absolute delight as Mr Allwit' and called Matthew Scurfield's Mr Yellowhammer 'impure gold' (1 September). David Benedict of the *Independent* commented on the doubling – McKay used male actors in drag as gossips in the christening scene, whereas in the original production they would have been boys – and ended his review by saying 'McKay takes a crude play in what seems like a crude theatre and translates it into a treasurable event' (5 September). Lyn Gardner was more critical in the *Guardian*: 'a lot of the jokes and performances are over-laboured. Middleton wasn't writing broad farce but very precise satire ... the effect of the production is to make the play seem more Dickensian than Jacobean, and create a gallery of loveable (sic) rogues rather than a cast of despicable villains who'd happily slit your throat on a dark night and enjoy watching you bleed to death. This is all too pleasant by half. You miss the sour stench of Middleton's poisonous humour' (1 September). While agreeing that 'Middleton's evocation of Jacobean London, with prowling adventurers, cuckolding and sex everywhere, could be more biting,' the *Times* critic, Benedict Nightingale, added that the play 'still comes over as a gorgeously funny romp', and made it his Critic's Choice of the week (12 September).

Note on the Text

The Lord Chamberlain, Sir Henry Herbert, licensed the play for publication on 8 April 1630 and it was printed in quarto in the same year, probably by the brothers Thomas and Richard Cotes. This is the only known early edition; twenty copies are accessible and the present text has been prepared from a collation of the copy in the State Library of South Australia and photographic reproductions of those in the Library of Congress and the Henry E. Huntington, Folger and Harvard University libraries. (The State Library of South Australia lacks sig. K4; the Harvard copy is lacking the K gathering and the lower part of sig. I4). A Xerox print of the Huntington copy was used as the working text.

The few variants which occur in no way affect the meaning, but indicate that corrections were made as the play was going through the press. Pages 50, 51, 54 and 55 (sigs. H1v, H2r, H3v and H4r) are incorrectly numbered 36, 33, 40 and 37 in the Folger and Library of Congress copies, for example, while the Harvard, Huntington and State Library of South Australia copies are paginated correctly, indicating that they were printed later in the run.

Over two centuries elapsed before the play appeared again, edited by Alexander Dyce (*The Works of Thomas Middleton*, vol. iv, London, 1840), A. H. Bullen (*The Works of Thomas Middleton*, vol. v, London, 1885–86), which is virtually a reprint of Dyce's, and Havelock Ellis (*Thomas Middleton*, vol. i, London, 1887) for the earlier Mermaid series, based on a collation of those of Dyce and Bullen. Inconsistent in their modernization, cavalier in their treatment of the verse, and laborious in their punctuation, these nineteenth-century editions at least made this play, and many others, accessible to the student and the general reader. The 1968 New Mermaid was the first twentieth-century edition; this was followed by five others, the most important R. B. Parker's for the Revels series, with a richly informative introduction and wonderfully detailed, if sometimes over-imaginative, notes.

The quarto seems to have been printed from a carefully prepared manuscript; it has few of the contractions and punctuation peculiar to Middleton's own hand[23] and except in one place it does not appear to be very close to the prompt book. The one instance is the long direction for the entry of the lovers' funeral (V.iv). The list of characters, the careful act divisions and the general tidiness of the text argue for the preparation of a scribal copy especially for the printing house. Both Parker and Charles Barber in his Fountainwell Drama Texts edition (Edinburgh, 1969) agree that the copytext for the printer was most likely a scribal copy of Middleton's autograph manuscript which had passed through the censor's hands but not been prepared for the playhouse; Parker also thinks that it was not prepared for the printing house.

Punctuation in the quarto relies much on the comma and on capitalization. There are relatively few full stops. The effect gained is one of lively conversational speech. While this kind of punctuation works well when the lines are spoken aloud, and so argues for a close relation to a dramatic text, it can offer some difficulty when read on the page. I have tried to preserve the original vitality by punctuating lightly, and while the quarto consistently uses a vocative capital (e.g. 'How is't with you Sir?'; V.i.36), I have decapitalized but not inserted a vocative comma except where its absence would impair the sense. Also in the interests of pace I have retained the contractions and elisions which occur throughout the play.

---

[23] See Middleton, *A Game at Chesse*, ed. R. C. Bald (Cambridge, 1929), pp. 34, 171–3.

Names are normalized and speech prefixes expanded, oaths are reg-
ularized without an apostrophe ('Foot', not "Foot') and all lines of
verse begin with capitals.

The quarto has no scene divisions but gives Latin headings for the
acts, from *Actus Primus* to *Actus Quintus*; these become Act I, Act
II and so on. Editorial stage directions and other additions are
enclosed in square brackets, *Ex[eunt]* indicating that the quarto has
Exit used inappropriately. While Middleton's characters address
the audience on many occasions, to keep the text as unencumbered
as possible editorial insertion of *Aside* has been kept to a minimum.
The reader or actor can quickly work out to whom a speech or part
of a speech is to be directed.

FURTHER READING

R. H. Barker, *Thomas Middleton*, New York, 1958

M. C. Bradbrook, *The Growth and Structure of Elizabethan
Comedy*, 1955

A. G. van den Broek, 'Take the Number Seven in Cheapside', *SEL*,
28 (1988), 319–30

H. R. Burke, 'The Kaleidoscopic Vision: Multiple Perspectives in
Middleton's *A Chaste Maid in Cheapside*', *Iowa State Journal of
Research*, 57 (1982), 123–9

A. Covatta, *Thomas Middleton's City Comedies*, Lewisburg, 1973

S. Chakravorty, *Society and Politics in the Plays of Thomas
Middleton*, Oxford, 1996

R. Chatterji, 'Theme, Imagery and Unity in *A Chaste Maid in
Cheapside*', *Renaissance Drama*, 8 (1965), 105–26

U. M. Ellis-Fermor, *The Jacobean Drama*, rev. edn, 1961

D. M. Farr, *Thomas Middleton and the Drama of Realism*,
Edinburgh, 1973

K. Friedenreich, ed., *'Accompaninge the Players': Essays
Celebrating Thomas Middleton, 1580–1980*, New York, 1983

D. George, 'Thomas Middleton's Sources: A Survey', *N&Q*, 18
(1971), 17–24

B. Gibbons, *Jacobean City Comedy*, 2nd edn, 1980

M. Heinemann, *Puritanism and Theatre: Thomas Middleton and
Opposition Drama Under the Early Stuarts*, Cambridge, 1980

D. M. Holmes, *The Art of Thomas Middleton*, Oxford, 1970

L. C. Knights, *Drama and Society in the Age of Jonson*, 1937

D. J. Lake, *The Canon of Thomas Middleton's Plays: Internal
Evidence for the Major Problems of Authorship*, 1975

R. Levin, *The Multiple Plot in English Renaissance Drama*, Chicago, 1971

A. F. Marotti, 'Fertility and Comic Form in *A Chaste Maid in Cheapside*', *Comparative Drama*, 3 (1969), 65–74

T. Middleton, *A Game at Chesse*, ed. R. C. Bald, Cambridge, 1929
Hengist, King of Kent, ed. R. C. Bald, New York, 1938

R. B. Parker, 'Middleton's Experiments with Comedy and Judgement', in *Jacobean Theatre*, ed. J. R. Brown and B. Harris, 1960

G. K. Paster, 'Leaky Vessels: The Incontinent Women of City Comedy', *Renaissance Drama*, 18 (1987), 43–65

M. Roberts, 'Productions of Middleton's Plays', *RORD*, 28 (1985), 45–7

G. E. Rowe, Jr., *Thomas Middleton and the New Comedy Tradition*, Lincoln, 1979

E. Schafer, 'Census of Renaissance Drama Productions', *RORD*, 37 (1998), 72–3

S. Schoenbaum, *Middleton's Tragedies*, New York, 1955
'*A Chaste Maid in Cheapside* and Middleton's City Comedy', in *Studies in the English Renaissance Drama*, ed. J. W. Bennett *et al.*, New York, 1959
'*Hengist King of Kent* and Sexual Preoccupation in Jacobean Drama', *PQ*, 29 (1950), 182–98

G. B. Shand, 'The Naming of Sir Walter Whorehound', *N&Q*, 29 (1982), 136–7

G. U. de Sousa, 'Thomas Middleton: Criticism since T. S. Eliot', *RORD*, 28 (1985), 73–83

S. J. Steen, *Thomas Middleton: A Reference Guide*, Boston, 1984
'The Response to Middleton: His Own Time to Eliot', *RORD*, 28 (1985), 63–71.

S. Wigler, 'Thomas Middleton's *A Chaste Maid in Cheapside*: The Delicious and the Disgusting', *American Imago*, 33 (1976), 195–215.

R. I. Williams, 'Machiavelli's *Mandragola*, Touchwood Senior, and the Comedy of Middleton's *A Chaste Maid in Cheapside*', *SEL*, 10 (1970), 385–96.

Note. The place of publication of books mentioned throughout this edition is London unless stated otherwise.

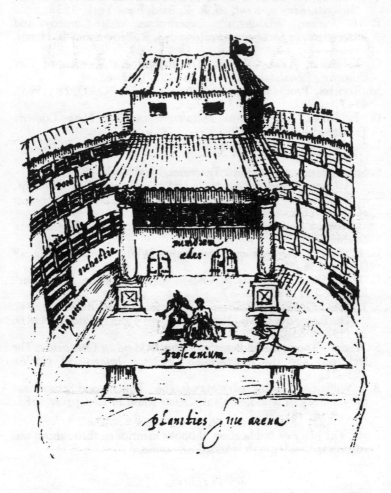

Sketch of the Swan Theatre (Utrecht University Library, MS 842, fol. 132r). See Introduction p. xxvii and the note on p. 2.

A

CHAST MAYD

IN

CHEAPE-SIDE.

A

Pleasant conceited Comedy
neuer before printed.

As it hath beene often acted at the
Swan on the Banke-side, by the
Lady ELIZABETH her
Seruants.

By THOMAS MIDBLTON Gent.

LONDON,
Printed for *Francis Constable* dwelling at the
signe of the *Crane* in *Pauls*
Church-yard.
1630.

The Original Title Page

Title page of the quarto edition (reproduced by permission of the Huntington Library, San Marino, California).

The title is paradoxical, and perhaps proverbial: 'A chaste maid in Cheapside? Not likely!'

conceited ingenious, clever

the Swan theatre stood in Paris Garden on the Bankside; built probably in 1596, used irregularly for plays and other entertainments until 1620 and still standing, though ruinous, in 1632. The inside was sketched by a Dutch visitor, Johannes de Witt, about 1596; a copy of this sketch, made by Aernout (or Arend) van Buchell, was found in the Utrecht University Library and published in 1888; it is the only known contemporary representation of an Elizabethan public playhouse interior.

Lady Elizabeth her Servants were a company of adult players active 1611–16 in London, 1612–22 in the provinces, 1622–5 in London. Revived in 1628 as the Queen of Bohemia's Players, they continued until about 1641. The Lady Elizabeth, the eldest daughter of James I, was born in 1596, married Frederick V, Elector Palatine, in 1613, became Queen of Bohemia in 1619, and died in 1662.

Paul's Churchyard was the centre of the London book trade. There were two classes of business premises around the cathedral church, houses which bordered the churchyards, and less substantial booths (or lock-up shops) and stalls clustered round the walls and at the doors of the building itself.

The Names of the Principal Persons

MR contraction for 'Master'; the modern 'Mister' came into general use later in the 17th century

YELLOWHAMMER (a) referring to his goldsmith's trade (b) a bird (c) slang for 'a gold coin' (d) a term of contempt, a fool

MAUDLINE pronounced and also spelt 'Maudlin' (a) Magdalene; traditionally Mary Magdalene, the friend of Jesus, was a reformed prostitute, but there is no evidence for this in the Bible (b) mawkish, sentimental

TIM Used by Jonson as a term of contempt: 'you are an otter, and a shad, a whit, / A very tim' (*The Alchemist* IV.vii.45–6); as an otter is 'neither fish not flesh' (*I Henry IV*, III.iii.127), a shad is a fish of the herring family, and a whit is the least part of something, 'Tim' also implies 'small'. See IV.i.123.

MOLL (a) diminutive of 'Mary' (b) slang for 'whore'; a prime example of Middleton's ambiguous use of names

THE NAMES OF THE PRINCIPAL PERSONS

MR YELLOWHAMMER, a goldsmith
MAUDLINE, his wife
TIM, their son
MOLL, their daughter
TUTOR to Tim
SIR WALTER WHOREHOUND, a suitor to Moll
SIR OLIVER KIX, and his WIFE, kin to Sir Walter
MR ALLWIT, and his WIFE, whom Sir Walter keeps
WELSH GENTLEWOMAN, Sir Walter's whore
WAT and NICK, his bastards [by Mrs Allwit]
DAVY DAHUMMA, his man
TOUCHWOOD SENIOR, and his WIFE, a decayed gentleman
TOUCHWOOD JUNIOR, another suitor to Moll
2 PROMOTERS
SERVANTS
WATERMEN
[PORTER
GENTLEMAN
COUNTRY WENCH, with a child
JUGG, maid to Lady Kix
DRY NURSE
WET NURSE

2 MEN, with baskets
MISTRESS UNDERMAN, a Puritan
PURITANS and GOSSIPS
MIDWIFE
PARSON
SUSAN, maid to Moll]

WALTER WHOREHOUND The name both describes the character's pursuit of sex and signifies his fecundity, as *Walter* was pronounced 'water' and 'water' was slang for semen (cf. II.i.188); moreover, the water horehound plant grows in moist, low places and medicine made from it induces childbirth.

OLIVER KIX While 'Oliver' = fruitful, 'Kix' = dry, hollow plant stem, figuratively a sapless person. Middleton had already used this name in *A Trick to Catch the Old One* (c. 1605).

ALLWIT a pun on 'Wittol' = a complaisant cuckold, but also (a) all cleverness (b) all penis

DAHUMMA 'Come hither' in Welsh (*dewch yma*)

TOUCHWOOD easily inflammable tinder, particularly that used to light a musket's touchhole; figuratively a passionate person (especially suitable when applied to Touchwood Junior)

PROMOTERS Originally a promoter was a lawyer, but by 1600 an informer; in Lent the authorities had promoters spying for butchers who sold meat without a licence.

WATERMEN Thames boatmen, the water taximen of the time

3

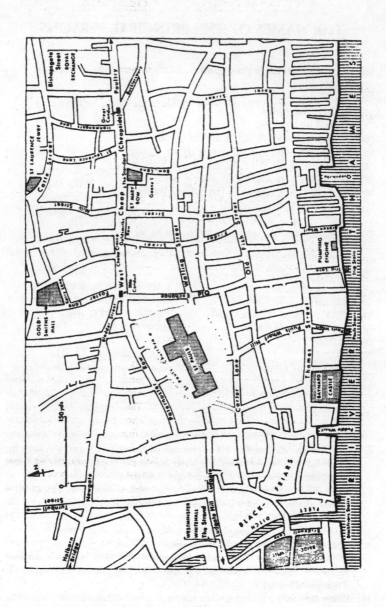

A CHASTE MAID IN CHEAPSIDE

Act I, [Scene i]

Enter MAUDLINE *and* MOLL, *a shop being discovered*

MAUDLINE
Have you played over all your old lessons o'the virginals?
MOLL
Yes.
MAUDLINE
Yes, you are a dull maid a-late, methinks you had need
have somewhat to quicken your green sickness; do you
weep? A husband! Had not such a piece of flesh been   5
ordained, what had us wives been good for? To make
salads, or else cried up and down for samphire. To see the
difference of these seasons! When I was of your youth, I
was lightsome, and quick, two years before I was married.
You fit for a knight's bed – drowsy browed, dull eyed,   10
drossy sprited – I hold my life you have forgot your dancing: when was the dancer with you?
MOLL
The last week.

Act I Q divides the play into acts only: scene numbers were added by Dyce
0 s.d. *discovered* Current scholarship increasingly tends to the view that a central
     entrance, in which such a discovery could be made, was usual in Elizabethan
     theatres; none is shown on the de Witt sketch. This direction, then, is possible
     evidence for a structure being built on the stage when needed, and/or a drawable
     curtain being hung from the overhang of the first gallery. See Introduction
     p. xxvii and V.iv.0 s.d. and note.
1 *virginals* small, legless keyboard instrument with plucked strings; playing it was
     a lady-like art which could easily give rise to sexual innuendo, as here
4 *green sickness* chlorosis; anaemic disease mostly affecting young women in
     puberty, giving them a pale or greenish complexion
6–7 *make salads* become salads (which, as they were highly seasoned, were related
     to lechery)
7 *cried . . . samphire* sold in the streets like samphire, a name given to two unre-
     lated plants, one used in salads, the other pickled and eaten with meat, particu-
     larly good with marsh mutton (cf. note to I.i.140)
9 *quick* (1) high spirited (2) pregnant
11 *sprited* spirited
11–12 *dancing* was popular with all classes, and London dancing schools were a
     sight for visitors; the sexual innuendo in Maudline's reminiscences is plain

MAUDLINE
>   Last week? When I was of your bord, he missed me not a
>   night, I was kept at it; I took delight to learn, and he to   15
>   teach me; pretty brown gentleman, he took pleasure in my
>   company; but you are dull, nothing comes nimbly from
>   you, you dance like a plumber's daughter, and deserve two
>   thousand pound in lead to your marriage, and not in gold-
>   smith's ware.   20

Enter YELLOWHAMMER

YELLOWHAMMER
>   Now what's the din betwixt mother and daughter, ha?

MAUDLINE
>   Faith small, telling your daughter Mary of her errors.

YELLOWHAMMER
>   'Errors'! Nay, the city cannot hold you wife, but you must
>   needs fetch words from Westminster; I ha' done i'faith. Has
>   no attorney's clerk been here a-late and changed his half-   25
>   crown-piece his mother sent him, or rather cozened you
>   with a gilded twopence, to bring the word in fashion for her
>   faults or cracks in duty and obedience? Term 'em e'en so,
>   sweet wife. As there is no woman made without a flaw,
>   your purest lawns have frays, and cambrics bracks.   30

MAUDLINE
>   But 'tis a husband solders up all cracks.

MOLL
>   What, is he come sir?

14 *bord* bore of a gun; 'when I was like you', with a pun on vaginal size
24 *Westminster* where justice was dispensed; Henry III ordered that the great hall
    at Westminster should be 'the usual place of pleadings, and ministration of jus-
    tice' (*Survey*, II, 117). Yellowhammer is saying, 'Has no attorney's clerk from
    Westminster been here lately to bribe you into using a highfalutin word (*errors*)
    for your daughter's faults? Isn't the ordinary language of the city good enough
    for you?'
25–6 *half-crown-piece* made of 22 carat gold, struck only in the last coinage of
    Henry VIII and one coinage of Elizabeth
26 *cozened* tricked
27 *gilded twopence* Twopenny pieces were of silver like all coins worth a shilling or
    less. If this one were treated to look like gold it would be counterfeit.
30 *lawns* fine linen or clothing made from it; so called because it was bleached on a
    lawn instead of the ordinary bleaching grounds
    cambrics a kind of white fine linen, originally made at Cambrai in France, or
    clothing made from it
    bracks flaws, faults, openings. This whole passage is innuendo.

YELLOWHAMMER   Sir Walter's come.
　He was met at Holborn Bridge, and in his company
　A proper fair young gentlewoman, which I guess
　By her red hair, and other rank descriptions,   35
　To be his landed niece brought out of Wales,
　Which Tim our son (the Cambridge boy) must marry.
　'Tis a match of Sir Walter's own making
　To bind us to him, and our heirs for ever.

MAUDLINE
　We are honoured then, if this baggage would be humble,   40
　And kiss him with devotion when he enters.
　I cannot get her for my life
　To instruct her hand thus, before and after,
　Which a knight will look for, before and after.
　I have told her still, 'tis the waving of a woman   45
　Does often move a man, and prevails strongly.
　But sweet, ha' you sent to Cambridge,
　Has Tim word on't?

YELLOWHAMMER
　Had word just the day after when you sent him the silver
　spoon to eat his broth in the hall, amongst the gentlemen   50
　commoners.

MAUDLINE
　O, 'twas timely.

Enter PORTER

YELLOWHAMMER
　How now?

PORTER
　A letter from a gentleman in Cambridge.

33　*Holborn Bridge* ancient bridge over the Fleet Ditch carrying the main road from
　　the west to enter London at Newgate
35　*rank* (1) abundant (2) lecherous (3) covered with coarse grass; red hair was
　　linked with lustfulness
43　*her hand* probably a fashionable way of carrying the hand before and behind the
　　body, but here with a sexual innuendo in 'before and after'
45　*still* constantly
　　waving (a) hand movement (b) body movement up and down
50　*hall* dining hall shared by students and members of a college
50–51　*gentlemen commoners* a privileged class of undergraduates at Oxford and
　　Cambridge, who wore a special gown and velvet cap, dined at a separate table
　　and paid higher fees

YELLOWHAMMER
> O, one of Hobson's porters: thou art welcome. I told thee   55
> Maud we should hear from Tim. [Reads] *Amantissimis*
> *charissimisque ambobus parentibus patri et matri.*

MAUDLINE
> What's the matter?

YELLOWHAMMER
> Nay by my troth, I know not, ask not me, he's grown too
> verbal; this learning is a great witch.   60

MAUDLINE
> Pray let me see it, I was wont to understand him.
> *Amantissimus charissimus*, he has sent the carrier's man, he
> says: *ambobus parentibus*, for a pair of boots: *patri et*
> *matri*, pay the porter, or it makes no matter.

PORTER
> Yes by my faith mistress, there's no true construction in   65
> that; I have took a great deal of pains, and come from the
> Bell sweating. Let me come to't, for I was a scholar forty
> years ago; 'tis thus I warrant you: *Matri*, it makes no
> matter: *ambobus parentibus*, for a pair of boots: *patri* pay
> the porter: *amantissimis charissimis*, he's the carrier's man,   70
> and his name is Sims, and there he says true, forsooth my
> name is Sims indeed; I have not forgot all my learning. A
> money matter, I thought I should hit on't.

YELLOWHAMMER
> Go thou art an old fox, there's a tester for thee.

---

55   *Hobson* (1544?–1631) the famous carrier of Cambridge who gave no alternative
     choice to those hiring his horses and so gave rise to the phrase 'Hobson's choice'
     (though this has been held to be a Cambridge hoax); from 1570 to 1630 his large
     six- and eight-horse wagons carried goods and mail between Cambridge and
     London; he died very rich and Milton wrote two epitaphs on him.
     thou Yellowhammer addresses the porter as an inferior. See Introduction p. xx.
     thee the familiar, affectionate use

56–7   'To my most loving and dearest parents, both father and mother'. Dyce and
     Bullen correct the Latin throughout the play, but as in some places the gram-
     matical mistakes indicate a greater foolishness the original has been retained in
     this edition, with modernized spelling.

58   *matter* content; but perhaps also 'What's the matter with you that you speak
     nonsense?'

65   *no true construction* inaccurate construing, translation; the porter's is just as
     comically bad

67   *Bell* Almost certainly a misprint for 'Bull', the inn on the western side of
     Bishopsgate which was Hobson's place of call.

74   *tester* sixpence (slang). First applied to the shilling of Henry VII but this became
     debased and the value fell.

PORTER

If I see your worship at Goose Fair, I have a dish of birds   75
for you.

YELLOWHAMMER

Why, dost dwell at Bow?

PORTER

All my lifetime sir I could ever say Bo, to a goose.
Farewell to your worship.   *Exit* PORTER

YELLOWHAMMER

A merry porter.   80

MAUDLINE

How can he choose but be so, coming with Cambridge letters from our son Tim?

YELLOWHAMMER

What's here? *Maximus diligo*. Faith I must to my learned
counsel with this gear – 'twill ne'er be discerned else.

MAUDLINE

Go to my cousin then, at Inns of Court.   85

YELLOWHAMMER

Fie, they are all for French, they speak no Latin.

MAUDLINE

The parson then will do it.

Enter a GENTLEMAN *with chain*

YELLOWHAMMER

Nay, he disclaims it, calls Latin Papistry; he will not deal
with it. What is't you lack, gentleman?

GENTLEMAN

Pray weigh this chain.   90

---

75 *Goose Fair* held annually on the Thursday after Whitsunday at Stratford le Bow,
   four miles northeast of St Paul's, where young (green) roast geese were sold;
   'goose' was also slang for a prostitute, so *a dish of birds* is probably said with a
   leer

78 *Bo, to a goose* proverbial. In Hollar's panorama of London (1647) Bow Church
   in the city is labelled 'Boo'. As 'bow' = cunt (see Introduction p. xxi) and 'goose'
   = whore, the porter is also making a bawdy joke.

83 Tim presumably means 'I esteem you most highly'; his Latin is more like 'I love
   you and I am the greatest'.

84 *gear* matter, stuff

85 *Inns of Court* Houses of law students, 'a whole university, as it were, of students,
   practisers or pleaders and Judges of the laws' (*Survey*, I, 76); Lincoln's Inn,
   Gray's Inn, the Inner Temple and the Middle Temple were the most important
   of the fourteen in 1603.

86 *French* The mongrel language known as 'Law French' continued in use for centuries in England; finally abolished by an act of Parliament in 1731.

Enter SIR WALTER WHOREHOUND, WELSH
GENTLEWOMAN *and* DAVY DAHUMMA

SIR WALTER
Now wench thou art welcome to the heart of the city of
London.

WELSH GENTLEWOMAN
Dugat a whee.

SIR WALTER
You can thank me in English if you list.

WELSH GENTLEWOMAN
I can sir, simply.   95

SIR WALTER
'Twill serve to pass wench; 'twas strange that I should lie
with thee so often, to leave thee without English – that were
unnatural. I bring thee up to turn thee into gold, wench,
and make thy fortune shine like your bright trade. A goldsmith's shop sets out a city maid. Davy Dahumma, not a   100
word.

DAVY
Mum, mum sir.

SIR WALTER
Here you must pass for a pure virgin.

DAVY
[*Aside*] Pure Welsh virgin! She lost her maidenhead in
Brecknockshire.   105

SIR WALTER
I hear you mumble Davy.

DAVY
I have teeth sir, I need not mumble yet this forty years.

SIR WALTER
The knave bites plaguily.

YELLOWHAMMER
What's your price sir?

GENTLEMAN
A hundred pound sir.   110

93 'God preserve you' – a phonetic rendering of '*Duw cadw chwi*'
96 '*twas strange that* it would be strange if
97 *thee* affectionate use
99 *your* impersonal 'one's', *bright trade* referring to goldsmith's trade, but possibly
personal, and referring to prostitution
102 *Mum* cant term, sign of silence and secrecy
105 *Brecknockshire* Welsh county; 'nock' was one of the many slang words for the
female genitals

YELLOWHAMMER
A hundred marks the utmost, 'tis not for me else.

                                        [*Exit* GENTLEMAN]

What, Sir Walter Whorehound?
MOLL
O death.   *Exit* MOLL
MAUDLINE
Why daughter;
Faith, the baggage,   115

                [*Exit* YELLOWHAMMER *after* MOLL]

A bashful girl sir; these young things are shamefast,
Besides, you have a presence, sweet Sir Walter,
Able to daunt a maid brought up i'the city;

            Enter MOLL [*brought back by* YELLOWHAMMER]

A brave Court spirit makes our virgins quiver,
And kiss with trembling thighs. Yet see she comes sir.   120
SIR WALTER
Why how now pretty mistress, now I have caught you.
What, can you injure so your time to stray thus from your
faithful servant?
YELLOWHAMMER
Pish, stop your words good knight, 'twill make her blush
else, which wound too high for the daughters of the   125
freedom. 'Honour', and 'faithful servant', they are
compliments for the worthies of Whitehall, or Greenwich.
E'en plain, sufficient subsidy words serves us sir. And is this
gentlewoman your worthy niece?

111 *marks* 1 mark was worth 13 shillings and 4 pence
116 *shamefast* bashful, modest
118 s.d. MOLL ed. (Mary Q). Unlikely to return voluntarily, perhaps Moll is brought
    back by her father.
120 *trembling thighs* A plain reference to the lasciviousness of the court; a 'knee-
    trembler' was coitus in a standing position. Romeo's Rosaline had a 'quivering
    thigh' (*Romeo and Juliet*, II.i.19).
125 *wound* past tense of 'wind' = go, but possibly a misprint for 'sound'
125–6 *daughters of the freedom* of the city of London as opposed to the court
127 *Whitehall* a royal palace from 1529 when Henry VIII took it from Cardinal
    Wolsey; it lay east of Westminster
    Greenwich ancient royal palace on the south bank of the Thames below London;
    birthplace of Henry VIII, Mary I and Elizabeth I
128 *subsidy* business, in this case commercial as opposed to courtly

SIR WALTER
  You may be bold with her on these terms, 'tis she sir, heir   130
  to some nineteen mountains.
YELLOWHAMMER
  Bless us all, you overwhelm me sir with love and riches.
SIR WALTER
  And all as high as Paul's.
DAVY
  Here's work i'faith.
SIR WALTER
  How sayst thou Davy?   135
DAVY
  Higher sir by far, you cannot see the top of 'em.
YELLOWHAMMER
  What, man? Maudline salute this gentlewoman, our daugh-
  ter if things hit right.

Enter TOUCHWOOD JUNIOR

TOUCHWOOD JUNIOR
  My knight with a brace of footmen
  Is come and brought up his ewe mutton   140
  To find a ram at London; I must hasten it,
  Or else pick a famine; her blood's mine,
  And that's the surest. Well knight, that choice spoil
  Is only kept for me.
MOLL
  Sir?   145
TOUCHWOOD JUNIOR
  Turn not to me till thou mayst lawfully, it but whets my
  stomach, which is too sharp set already. Read that note
  carefully, keep me from suspicion still, nor know my zeal

133 *as high as Paul's* proverbial. The cathedral tower was 245 feet (74 m) high; the
    steeple which surmounted it for another 205 feet (64 m) was destroyed by fire in
    1561.
135 *thou* Allwit consistently addresses Davy as a servant.
137 *salute* kiss
140 *ewe mutton* strumpet
142 *pick a famine* choose to starve. Some eds incorrectly emend 'peak a'famine', i.e.
    'dwindle from starvation'.
    blood passion (but also with a hunting connotation); 'She desires me sexually,
    and that ensures she'll be mine'
143 *spoil* ed. (spoy Q) prey. Another hunting image cf. IV.ii.102.
146 *thou* intimate, affectionate use
147 *sharp set* eager, keen

but in thy heart: read and send but thy liking in three
words, I'll be at hand to take it.   150
YELLOWHAMMER
O turn sir, turn.
A poor plain boy, an university man
Proceeds next Lent to a Bachelor of Art;
He will be called Sir Yellowhammer then
Over all Cambridge, and that's half a knight.   155
MAUDLINE
Please you draw near, and taste the welcome of the city sir?
YELLOWHAMMER
Come good Sir Walter, and your virtuous niece here.
SIR WALTER
'Tis manners to take kindness.
YELLOWHAMMER
Lead 'em in wife.
SIR WALTER
Your company sir.   160
YELLOWHAMMER
I'll give't you instantly.

    [*Exeunt* SIR WALTER, WELSH GENTLEWOMAN, DAVY *and*
                                 MAUDLINE]

TOUCHWOOD JUNIOR
How strangely busy is the devil and riches;
Poor soul kept in too hard, her mother's eye
Is cruel toward her, being to him.
'Twere a good mirth now to set him a-work   165
To make her wedding ring. I must about it.
Rather than the game should fall to a stranger,
'Twas honesty in me to enrich my father.
YELLOWHAMMER
The girl is wondrous peevish; I fear nothing

149 *liking* (1) consent, approval (2) sexual desire
151 *turn* Some eds emend 'Tim', but Yellowhammer is trying to persuade Sir Walter
    to enter his house, while telling him about Tim; Maudline adds her invitation at
    l. 156.
153 *Proceeds* Graduates (strictly, to a degree higher than Bachelor)
    Art could signify Yellowhammer's ignorance, but Dekker uses 'Bachelor of Art'
    without humorous intent in *The Gull's Hornbook* (1609, p. 9)
154 *Sir* was a rendering of Latin *dominus*. Used with the surname only it indicated
    an Oxford or Cambridge graduate, considered a member of the gentry; so, only
    half a knight.
164 *being to him* Turned to Whorehound, supporting Yellowhammer in arranging
    for Moll to marry the knight.

But that she's taken with some other love;   170
Then all's quite dashed: that must be narrowly looked to;
We cannot be too wary in our children.
What is't you lack?

TOUCHWOOD JUNIOR
O nothing now, all that I wish is present. I would have a
wedding ring made for a gentlewoman, with all speed that   175
may be.

YELLOWHAMMER
Of what weight sir?

TOUCHWOOD JUNIOR
Of some half ounce, stand fair and comely, with the spark
of a diamond. Sir 'twere pity to lose the least grace.

YELLOWHAMMER
Pray let's see it; indeed sir 'tis a pure one.   180

TOUCHWOOD JUNIOR
So is the mistress.

YELLOWHAMMER
Have you the wideness of her finger sir?

TOUCHWOOD JUNIOR
Yes sure I think I have her measure about me –
Good faith 'tis down, I cannot show't you,
I must pull too many things out to be certain.   185
Let me see, long, and slender, and neatly jointed,
Just such another gentlewoman that's your daughter sir.

YELLOWHAMMER
And therefore sir no gentlewoman.

TOUCHWOOD JUNIOR
I protest I never saw two maids handed more alike;
I'll ne'er seek farther, if you'll give me leave sir.   190

YELLOWHAMMER
If you dare venture by her finger sir.

TOUCHWOOD JUNIOR
Ay, and I'll bide all loss sir.

YELLOWHAMMER
Say you so sir, let's see hither girl.

179 *diamond* Wedding rings were often in the form of two hands clasping a heart
made of a jewel, or a hoop, sometimes enamelled, with small gems, and a motto
engraved inside.

183 *measure* (1) her finger's size (2) his penis, which can measure her. Middleton uses
the sexual imagery of fingers and rings in several plays, most potently in *The
Changeling*.

184 *down* (1) too deep in his pocket (2) detumescent

187 *that's* as is

192 *I'll bide all loss* 'I'll still pay if I've made any mistake'

TOUCHWOOD JUNIOR
Shall I make bold with your finger gentlewoman?
MOLL
Your pleasure sir.   195
TOUCHWOOD JUNIOR
That fits her to a hair sir.
YELLOWHAMMER
What's your posy now sir?
TOUCHWOOD JUNIOR
Mass that's true, posy i'faith, e'en thus sir:
'Love that's wise, blinds parents' eyes'.
YELLOWHAMMER
How, how? If I may speak without offence sir,   200
I hold my life –
TOUCHWOOD JUNIOR
What sir?
YELLOWHAMMER
Go to, you'll pardon me?
TOUCHWOOD JUNIOR
Pardon you? Ay sir.
YELLOWHAMMER
Will you i'faith?   205
TOUCHWOOD JUNIOR
Yes faith I will.
YELLOWHAMMER
You'll steal away some man's daughter, am I near you?
Do you turn aside? You gentlemen are mad wags;
I wonder things can be so warily carried,
And parents blinded so, but they're served right   210
That have two eyes, and wear so dull a sight.
TOUCHWOOD JUNIOR
[*Aside*] Thy doom take hold of thee.
YELLOWHAMMER
Tomorrow noon shall show your ring well done.
TOUCHWOOD JUNIOR
Being so 'tis soon; thanks, and your leave sweet gentle-
woman.   *Exit* 215

---

196 *to a hair* to perfection, with a pun on 'pubic hair', continuing on from *Your pleasure*
197 *posy* a motto, originally a line of verse or 'poesie', often inscribed inside a ring
198 *Mass* 'by the Mass', an oath
207 *am I near you?* 'do I guess your aim?' said with unconscious irony
211 *wear* (were Q); some editors emend 'were so dull a'sight, but cf. IV.ii.36 for a similar use of this spelling in Q

MOLL
   Sir you are welcome.
   [*Aside*] O were I made of wishes, I went with thee.
YELLOWHAMMER
   Come now we'll see how the rules go within.
MOLL
   That robs my joy, there I lose all I win.

                                                    Ex[*eunt*]

[Act I, Scene ii]

Enter DAVY *and* ALLWIT *severally*

DAVY
   Honesty wash my eyes, I have spied a wittol.
ALLWIT
   What, Davy Dahumma? Welcome from North Wales
   I'faith, and is Sir Walter come?
DAVY
   New come to town sir.
ALLWIT
   Into the maids sweet Davy, and give order his chamber be   5
   made ready instantly; my wife's as great as she can wallow
   Davy, and longs for nothing but pickled cucumbers, and his
   coming, and now she shall ha't boy.
DAVY
   She's sure of them sir.
ALLWIT
   Thy very sight will hold my wife in pleasure, till the knight   10
   come himself. Go in, in, in Davy.

                                                    Exit [DAVY]

   The founder's come to town! I am like a man
   Finding a table furnished to his hand,

218 *rules* revels; 'Tumultuous frolicsome conduct' (J. O. Halliwell, *Dictionary of Archaic and Provincial Words* (1874))

0 s.d. *severally* separately
7 *pickled cucumbers* made with verjuice, the sharp, slightly fermented juice of sour grapes or crab apples – pregnancy produces strange cravings; and this is a hidden irony, as 'pickled' = poxed and cucumbers are phallic
13 *table* Cf. Psalm 78:19 'Can God furnish a table?' and Proverbs 9:2 'Wisdom . . . hath mingled her wine; she hath also furnished her table' (*The Holy Bible*, 1611); blasphemy continues with *prays* and *bless*.

As mine is still to me, prays for the founder;
Bless the right worshipful, the good founder's life.   15
I thank him, h'as maintained my house this ten years,
Not only keeps my wife, but a keeps me,
And all my family; I am at his table,
He gets me all my children, and pays the nurse,
Monthly, or weekly, puts me to nothing,   20
Rent, nor church duties, not so much as the scavenger:
The happiest state that ever man was born to.
I walk out in a morning, come to breakfast,
Find excellent cheer, a good fire in winter,
Look in my coal house about midsummer eve,   25
That's full, five or six chaldron, new laid up;
Look in my back yard, I shall find a steeple
Made up with Kentish faggots, which o'erlooks
The waterhouse and the windmills; I say nothing
But smile, and pin the door. When she lies in,   30
As now she's even upon the point of grunting,
A lady lies not in like her; there's her embossings,
Embroiderings, spanglings, and I know not what,
As if she lay with all the gaudy shops
In Gresham's Burse about her; then her restoratives,   35
Able to set up a young 'pothecary,
And richly stock the foreman of a drug shop;

17 *a* he
18 *family* includes servants as well as children
21 *church . . . scavenger* Parish dues (*duties*) could be paid in cash or service. The
    scavenger was a town officer who employed the poor to sweep the streets and
    chimneys; Stow says Bread Street ward, which contained part of Cheapside, had
    eight.
26 *chaldron* a dry measure of 36 bushels of coal; the coal trade between Newcastle
    and London grew tenfold between 1545 and 1625 and while Shakespeare was in
    London the price per chaldron rose from four shillings to nine
28 *Kentish faggots* bundles of brushwood, about eight feet long (2.44 m) and a foot
    (30.5 cm) through; much London firewood came from Kent
29 *waterhouse and the windmills* either the house near Broken Wharf in which
    Bevis Bulmer in 1594 built an 'engine' 'to convey Thames water into men's
    houses of West Cheap, about Paul's, Fleet Street, &c' (*Survey*, I, 8) or Sir Hugh
    Middleton's recently completed reservoir in Islington; windmills could be seen to
    both north and south of Cheapside
30 *pin* bolt
35 *Gresham's Burse* the Royal Exchange, 'whose founder was Sir Thomas Gresham
    Knight, agent to her Majesty, built 1556–8 for the confluence and commerce of
    merchants' (John Speed, *The Theatre of . . . Great Britain* (1611), fol. 852)

Her sugar by whole loaves, her wines by rundlets.
I see these things, but like a happy man,
I pay for none at all, yet fools think's mine;   40
I have the name, and in his gold I shine.
And where some merchants would in soul kiss hell,
To buy a paradise for their wives, and dye
Their conscience in the bloods of prodigal heirs,
To deck their night-piece, yet all this being done,   45
Eaten with jealousy to the inmost bone –
As what affliction nature more constrains,
Than feed the wife plump for another's veins?
These torments stand I freed of, I am as clear
From jealousy of a wife as from the charge.   50
O two miraculous blessings; 'tis the knight
Hath took that labour all out of my hands;
I may sit still and play; he's jealous for me –
Watches her steps, sets spies – I live at ease;
He has both the cost and torment; when the strings   55
Of his heart frets, I feed, laugh, or sing,
La dildo, dildo la dildo, la dildo dildo de dildo.

Enter TWO SERVANTS

1 SERVANT
What has he got a-singing in his head now?
2 SERVANT
Now he's out of work he falls to making dildoes.
ALLWIT
Now sirs, Sir Walter's come.   60
1 SERVANT
Is our master come?

38 *rundlets* barrels; large rundlets held between 12 and 18½ gallons (54.6–84.2
    litres), small between a pint and four gallons (0.57–18.2 litres)
40 *think's* think it's
43–4 *dye . . . heirs* 'wickedly extort money from spendthrift sons of the gentry to
    buy clothing and jewellery for their whores'. Gulling 'prodigal heirs' is a major
    theme in Middleton's *Michaelmas Term* (c. 1606).
45 *night-piece* mistress, bedfellow
47 *nature more constrains* restricts nature more
55–6 *strings . . . frets* The heart was supposed to be braced with strings, which
    frayed and broke under emotional stress; the fret of a musical instrument was a
    ring of gut, now wood or metal, on the fingerboard to regulate fingering.
57 *dildo* This chorus has ironic overtones; a dildo is a substitute phallus.
58 *a-singing . . . head* reference to horns, the common insignia of the cuckold, a man
    with an adulterous wife
59 *work* sexual activity (slang)

ALLWIT
  Your master? What am I?
SERVANT
  Do not you know sir?
ALLWIT
  Pray am not I your master?
I SERVANT
  O you are but our mistress's husband.   65

Enter SIR WALTER *and* DAVY

ALLWIT
  Ergo knave, your master.
I SERVANT
  Negatur argumentum. Here comes Sir Walter, now a stands
  bare as well as we; make the most of him he's but one peep
  above a servingman, and so much his horns make him.
SIR WALTER
  How dost Jack?   70
ALLWIT
  Proud of your worship's health sir.
SIR WALTER
  How does your wife?
ALLWIT
  E'en after your own making sir,
  She's a tumbler i'faith, the nose and belly meets.
SIR WALTER
  They'll part in time again.   75
ALLWIT
  At the good hour, they will, and please your worship.
SIR WALTER
  Here sirrah, pull off my boots. Put on, put on Jack.
ALLWIT
  I thank your kind worship sir.
SIR WALTER
  Slippers! Heart, you are sleepy.

66 *Ergo* 'Therefore'
67 *Negatur argumentum* 'Your argument is denied'
68 *peep* pip, degree; from a card game 'one-and-thirty' in which thirty-two was 'a
   pip out', the pips being the spots on the cards
70 *Jack* This may well be Allwit's name, but it is also a generic name for (a) a low
   bred, common fellow (Sir Walter is asserting his authority immediately) (b) a
   penis.
74 *She's a tumbler . . . meets* 'She's a copulator, and she's pregnant'
77 *Put on* Hats were normally worn indoors; Allwit has removed his out of defer-
   ence.

ALLWIT
    The game begins already.   80

SIR WALTER
    Pish, put on, Jack.

ALLWIT
    Now I must do it, or he'll be as angry now as if I had put it
    on at first bidding; 'tis but observing, 'tis but observing a
    man's humour once, and he may ha' him by the nose all his
    life.   85

SIR WALTER
    What entertainment has lain open here?
    No strangers in my absence?

I SERVANT
    Sure sir not any.

ALLWIT
    His jealousy begins; am not I happy now
    That can laugh inward whilst his marrow melts?   90

SIR WALTER
    How do you satisfy me?

I SERVANT
    Good sir be patient.

SIR WALTER
    For two months' absence I'll be satisfied.

I SERVANT
    No living creature entered –

SIR WALTER
    Entered? Come swear –   95

I SERVANT
    You will not hear me out sir –

SIR WALTER
    Yes I'll hear't out sir.

I SERVANT
    Sir he can tell himself.

SIR WALTER   Heart he can tell!
    Do you think I'll trust him? As a usurer
    With forfeited lordships. Him, O monstrous injury!   100
    Believe him? Can the devil speak ill of darkness?
    What can you say sir?

---

84 *humour* disposition
    he one, you
90 *marrow melts* with the heat generated by his jealousy
100 *forfeited lordships* Mortgaged properties claimed by moneylenders for repay-
    ment of loans. A jibe at the low value of knighthood. Cf. note 43–4 above.

ALLWIT
Of my soul and conscience sir, she's a wife as honest of her
body to me as any lord's proud lady can be.

SIR WALTER
Yet, by your leave, I heard you were once offering to go to   105
bed to her.

ALLWIT
No, I protest sir.

SIR WALTER
Heart if you do, you shall take all – I'll marry.

ALLWIT
O I beseech you sir –

SIR WALTER
That wakes the slave, and keeps his flesh in awe.   110

ALLWIT
I'll stop that gap
Where e'er I find it open; I have poisoned
His hopes in marriage already –
Some old rich widows, and some landed virgins –

Enter two CHILDREN

And I'll fall to work still before I'll lose him,   115
He's yet too sweet to part from.

1 BOY
God-den father.

ALLWIT
Ha villain, peace.

2 BOY
God-den father.

ALLWIT
Peace bastard; should he hear 'em! These are two foolish   120
children, they do not know the gentleman that sits there.

SIR WALTER
Oh Wat, how dost Nick? Go to school,
Ply your books boys, ha?

ALLWIT
Where's your legs whoresons? They should kneel indeed if
they could say their prayers.   125

SIR WALTER
Let me see, stay,
How shall I dispose of these two brats now
When I am married? For they must not mingle
Amongst my children that I get in wedlock –

117 *God-den* 'Good evening', but used any time after noon
124 *legs* a bow

'Twill make foul work that, and raise many storms.   130
I'll bind Wat prentice to a goldsmith, my father
   Yellowhammer;
As fit as can be. Nick with some vintner; good, goldsmith
And vintner; there will be wine in bowls, i'faith.

Enter ALLWIT'S WIFE

MISTRESS ALLWIT
   Sweet knight
   Welcome; I have all my longings now in town,   135
   Now well-come the good hour.
SIR WALTER
   How cheers my mistress?
MISTRESS ALLWIT
   Made lightsome, e'en by him that made me heavy.
SIR WALTER
   Methinks she shows gallantly, like a moon at full sir.
ALLWIT
   True, and if she bear a male child, there's the man in the   140
   moon sir.
SIR WALTER
   'Tis but the boy in the moon yet, goodman calf.
ALLWIT
   There was a man, the boy had never been there else.
SIR WALTER
   It shall be yours sir.

[*Exeunt* MISTRESS ALLWIT *and* SIR WALTER]

ALLWIT
   No by my troth, I'll swear it's none of mine, let him that   145
   got it keep it. Thus do I rid myself of fear,
   Lie soft, sleep hard, drink wine, and eat good cheer. [*Exit*]

Act II, [Scene i]

Enter TOUCHWOOD SENIOR *and his* WIFE

MISTRESS TOUCHWOOD
   'Twill be so tedious sir to live from you,
   But that necessity must be obeyed.

138 *heavy* pregnant
142 *calf* blockhead. Another small but subtle irony, since a 'mooncalf' is also a false
   pregnancy.

TOUCHWOOD SENIOR
   I would it might not wife, the tediousness
   Will be the most part mine, that understand
   The blessings I have in thee; so to part,   5
   That drives the torment to a knowing heart;
   But as thou sayst, we must give way to need
   And live awhile asunder; our desires
   Are both too fruitful for our barren fortunes.
   How adverse runs the destiny of some creatures –   10
   Some only can get riches and no children,
   We only can get children and no riches;
   Then 'tis the prudent'st part to check our wills,
   And till our state rise, make our bloods lie still.
   [*Aside*] Life every year a child, and some years two,   15
   Besides drinkings abroad, that's never reckoned;
   This gear will not hold out.
MISTRESS TOUCHWOOD
   Sir, for a time, I'll take the courtesy of my uncle's house
   If you be pleased to like on't, till prosperity
   Look with a friendly eye upon our states.   20
TOUCHWOOD SENIOR
   Honest wife I thank thee; I ne'er knew
   The perfect treasure thou brought'st with thee more
   Than at this instant minute. A man's happy
   When he's at poorest that has matched his soul
   As rightly as his body. Had I married   25
   A sensual fool now, as 'tis hard to 'scape it
   'Mongst gentlewomen of our time, she would ha' hanged
   About my neck, and never left her hold
   Till she had kissed me into wanton businesses,
   Which at the waking of my better judgement   30
   I should have cursed most bitterly,
   And laid a thicker vengeance on my act
   Than misery of the birth, which were enough

---

  5 *blessings* (a) happiness (b) children. Cf. Shakespeare, 'bairns [i.e. children] are
     blessings', *All's Well* I.iii.25.
  7 *thou* Touchwood Senior uses the affectionate form to his wife, who, like most
     wives to their husbands, addresses him with 'you'.
 13 *wills* sexual desires
 14 *bloods* passions
 15 *Life* 'By God's life'. An Act for the 'preventing . . . of the great abuse of the Holy
     Name of God in Stage plays, interludes . . . and such like' was passed in May
     1606; offenders were liable for a fine of £10 for each lapse.
 16 *drinkings abroad* sexual adventures away from home
 17 *gear* (a) business (b) genitals

If it were born to greatness, whereas mine
Is sure of beggary, though it were got in wine.   35
Fullness of joy showeth the goodness in thee –
Thou art a matchless wife; farewell my joy.

MISTRESS TOUCHWOOD
I shall not want your sight?

TOUCHWOOD SENIOR   I'll see thee often,
Talk in mirth, and play at kisses with thee,
Anything wench but what may beget beggars;   40
There I give o'er the set, throw down the cards,
And dare not take them up.

MISTRESS TOUCHWOOD   Your will be mine sir.   *Exit*

TOUCHWOOD SENIOR
This does not only make her honesty perfect,
But her discretion, and approves her judgement.
Had her desires been wanton, they'd been blameless   45
In being lawful ever, but of all creatures
I hold that wife a most unmatched treasure
That can unto her fortunes fix her pleasure,
And not unto her blood – this is like wedlock;
The feast of marriage is not lust but love,   50
And care of the estate. When I please blood,
Merely I sing, and suck out others'; then,
'Tis many a wise man's fault; but of all men
I am the most unfortunate in that game
That ever pleased both genders: I ne'er played yet   55
Under a bastard. The poor wenches curse me
To the pit where e'er I come; they were ne'er served so,
But used to have more words than one to a bargain.
I have such a fatal finger in such business
I must forth with't, chiefly for country wenches,   60
For every harvest I shall hinder hay-making;

Enter a WENCH *with a child*

---

41 *give o'er the set* abandon the game, as in dice, cards or tennis

44 *approves* confirms, attests

45 *desires* ed. (desire Q)

52 *sing* fuck; Parker suggests a misprint for 'sting', symbolizing lust as a flesh-fly,
    which links with *suck out others'* blood

    Merely . . . others' My slightest sexual activity always hurts somebody

55–6 *I . . . bastard* 'At the very least there's always a bastard'. A 'bastard card' is a
    single card left in a hand and which counts against the player.

58 *used to have more words than one to a bargain* assume they'd not get pregnant
    on the first encounter. 'More words . . . bargain' is proverbial for being unwill-
    ing to agree easily.

I had no less than seven lay in last Progress,
Within three weeks of one another's time.

WENCH

O Snaphance, have I found you?

TOUCHWOOD SENIOR   How Snaphance?

WENCH

Do you see your workmanship?   65
Nay turn not from it, nor offer to escape, for if you do,
I'll cry it through the streets, and follow you.
Your name may well be called Touchwood, a pox on you,
You do but touch and take; thou hast undone me;
I was a maid before, I can bring a certificate for it,   70
From both the churchwardens.

TOUCHWOOD SENIOR

I'll have the parson's hand too, or I'll not yield to't.

WENCH

Thou shalt have more, thou villain. Nothing grieves me, but
Ellen my poor cousin in Derbyshire, thou hast cracked her
marriage quite; she'll have a bout with thee.   75

TOUCHWOOD SENIOR

Faith when she will I'll have a bout with her.

WENCH

A law bout sir I mean.

TOUCHWOOD SENIOR

True, lawyers use such bouts as other men do,
And if that be all thy grief, I'll tender her a husband;
I keep of purpose two or three gulls in pickle   80

62 *Progress* Annual royal visit to various parts of the country, usually in July and
   August; expensive festivities and a holiday atmosphere were expected by the sov-
   ereign.

64 *Snaphance* Flintlock on guns or, more appropriately here, a musket or gun fitted
   with a flintlock. The flintlock ignited touchwood in a gun's touchhole – the
   sexual imagery is obvious.

69 *touch and take* proverbial
   thou The Wench is growing more angry with Touchwood Senior, and does not
   return to 'you' until l. 101.

71 *churchwardens* lay honorary officers who helped the incumbent of a parish; they
   could issue the character reference needed by everyone moving out of their own
   parish, though these were famously unreliable (cf. 'a certificate (such as rogues
   have) from the head men of the Parish', Thomas Nashe, *Strange News* (1592),
   sig. C4)

75 *bout* quarrel; taken up by Touchwood Senior in the sexual sense and used again
   in the legal sense

80 *in pickle* (a) in reserve (like preserved fruit or vegetables) (b) poxy, as the sweat-
   ing vats used for curing venereal disease were known as 'pickling tubs'

To eat such mutton with, and she shall choose one.
Do but in courtesy, faith, wench, excuse me
Of this half yard of flesh, in which I think it wants
A nail or two.

WENCH   No, thou shalt find villain
It hath right shape, and all the nails it should have.   85

TOUCHWOOD SENIOR
Faith I am poor; do a charitable deed wench,
I am a younger brother, and have nothing.

WENCH
Nothing! Thou hast too much thou lying villain
Unless thou wert more thankful.

TOUCHWOOD SENIOR   I have no dwelling,
I brake up house but this morning; pray thee pity me,   90
I am a good fellow, faith have been too kind
To people of your gender; if I ha't
Without my belly, none of your sex shall want it;
[Aside] That word has been of force to move a woman.
There's tricks enough to rid thy hand on't wench,   95
Some rich man's porch, tomorrow before day,
Or else anon i'the evening – twenty devices;
Here's all I have, i'faith, take purse and all,
[Aside] And would I were rid of all the ware i'the shop so.

WENCH
Where I find manly dealings I am pitiful;   100
This shall not trouble you.

TOUCHWOOD SENIOR
And I protest wench, the next I'll keep myself.

WENCH
Soft, let it be got first.
[Aside] This is the fifth; if e'er I venture more
Where I now go for a maid, may I ride for a whore.   Exit   105

80–81 *gulls . . . one* 'I keep a few fools for such whores and she can have one for a
    husband'
84 *nail* a measure of cloth, one sixteenth of a yard; here with a pun, as syphilitics'
    children sometimes lack fingernails
87 *younger brother* The custom of primogeniture, by which property and title
    descended to the first born, meant that younger sons often had to live by their
    wits. Touchwood Senior has an older brother, or else he's lying.
92–3 *if I . . . belly* (a) 'if I have uneaten food' (b) 'while I have a phallus'
97 *anon* straight away
99 *ware i'the shop* (a) all my other bastards (b) other whores
105 *ride* Being paraded in a cart was a punishment for whores; there is also a pun on
    straddling as a position in sexual intercourse.

TOUCHWOOD SENIOR
  What shift she'll make now with this piece of flesh
  In this strict time of Lent, I cannot imagine;
  Flesh dare not peep abroad now; I have known
  This city now above this seven years,
  But I protest in better state of government   110
  I never knew it yet, nor ever heard of;
  There has been more religious wholesome laws
  In the half circle of a year erected
  For common good, than memory ever knew of,

              Enter SIR OLIVER KIX *and his* LADY

  Setting apart corruption of promoters,   115
  And other poisonous officers that infect
  And with a venomous breath taint every goodness.
LADY KIX
  O that e'er I was begot, or bred, or born.
SIR OLIVER
  Be content sweet wife.
TOUCHWOOD SENIOR   What's here to do now?
  I hold my life she's in deep passion   120
  For the imprisonment of veal and mutton
  Now kept in garrets, weeps for some calf's head now;
  Methinks her husband's head might serve with bacon.

              Enter TOUCHWOOD JUNIOR

LADY KIX
  Hist.
SIR OLIVER
  Patience sweet wife.   125
TOUCHWOOD JUNIOR
  Brother I have sought you strangely.
TOUCHWOOD SENIOR
  Why, what's the business?

---

107 *Lent* the period in the Christian church from Ash Wednesday to Easter Eve, of
    which the 40 week-days are devoted to fasting and penitence in commemoration
    of Christ's 40 days in the Wilderness; see Introduction p. xxvi
122 *calf's head* also means a fool
124 *Hist* Some editors give this to Touchwood Junior but as it means 'Be quiet!' it is
    appropriate for Lady Kix, as in Q.
126 *you* Here a formal use by a younger brother before the familial *thou* of ll. 128
    and 131.
    strangely extremely; 'I've been looking hard for you'

TOUCHWOOD JUNIOR
  With all speed thou canst, procure a licence for me.
TOUCHWOOD SENIOR
  How, a licence?
TOUCHWOOD JUNIOR
  Cud's foot she's lost else, I shall miss her ever.   130
TOUCHWOOD SENIOR
  Nay sure thou shalt not miss so fair a mark
  For thirteen shillings fourpence.
TOUCHWOOD JUNIOR   Thanks by hundreds. *Exit*
SIR OLIVER
  Nay pray thee cease, I'll be at more cost yet,
  Thou know'st we are rich enough.
LADY KIX   All but in blessings,
  And there the beggar goes beyond us. O, O, O,   135
  To be seven years a wife and not a child, O not a child!
SIR OLIVER
  Sweet wife have patience.
LADY KIX
  Can any woman have a greater cut?
SIR OLIVER
  I know 'tis great, but what of that wife?
  I cannot 'do withal; there's things making   140
  By thine own doctor's advice at 'pothecary's;
  I spare for nothing wife, no, if the price
  Were forty marks a spoonful,
  I'd give a thousand pound to purchase fruitfulness
  'Tis but bating so many good works   145
  In the erecting of Bridewells and spital-houses,

128 *licence* Only the Archbishop of Canterbury could issue a licence for a marriage in a place other than a church or chapel; a licence was also necessary for a marriage for which banns had not been called.

130 *Cud's foot* a defanged oath, 'By God's foot'

131 *mark* target

132 *thirteen* value of a mark, the cost of a special marriage licence

133 *thee* Both Sir Oliver and Lady Kix use *thee* and *thou* denoting anger.

138 *cut* (a) misfortune (b) cunt

140 *do withal* (a) help it (b) fuck

145 *bating* diminishing

146 *Bridewells and spital-houses* Bridewell, originally a royal palace, was given to London by Edward VI 'to be a house of correction for lewd and dissolute livers' (Speed, *The Theatre of . . . Great Britain* (1611), fol. 814); here used for prisons in general. Spitals were hospitals, especially for leprosy and venereal disease.

And so fetch it up again – for having none
I mean to make good deeds my children.

LADY KIX
Give me but those good deeds, and I'll find children.

SIR OLIVER
Hang thee, thou hast had too many!   150

LADY KIX
Thou lie'st, brevity!

SIR OLIVER
O horrible, dar'st thou call me 'brevity'?
Dar'st thou be so short with me?

LADY KIX
Thou deservest worse.
Think but upon the goodly lands and livings   155
That's kept back through want on't.

SIR OLIVER
Talk not on't pray thee,
Thou'lt make me play the woman and weep too.

LADY KIX
'Tis our dry barrenness puffs up Sir Walter –
None gets by your not-getting, but that knight;   160
He's made by th'means, and fats his fortunes shortly
In a great dowry with a goldsmith's daughter.

                    [Exit TOUCHWOOD SENIOR]

SIR OLIVER
They may all be deceived,
Be but you patient wife.

LADY KIX
I have suffered a long time.   165

SIR OLIVER
Suffer thy heart out; a pox suffer thee!

LADY KIX
Nay thee, thou desertless slave!

SIR OLIVER
Come, come, I ha' done;
You'll to the gossiping of Master Allwit's child?

---

147 *fetch it up again* (a) 'if I can't buy fruitfulness I'll save the money and be a phil-
   anthropist' (b) 'I'll recover from sexual impotence'
162 s.d. Q has no exit for Touchwood Senior, but this would be an appropriate place
   for him to leave, having overheard the cause of the Kixes' quarrel and being
   reminded of his brother's marriage plans.
169 *gossiping* christening
   Master ed. (Q Mr). Parker reads 'Mistress' but the masculine is more appropriately ironic, given the recent argument.

LADY KIX
   Yes, to my much joy;   170
   Everyone gets before me – there's my sister
   Was married but at Bartholomew eve last,
   And she can have two children at a birth;
   O one of them, one of them would ha' served my turn.

SIR OLIVER
   Sorrow consume thee, thou art still crossing me,   175
   And know'st my nature.

Enter a MAID

MAID
   O mistress, weeping or railing,
   That's our house harmony.

LADY KIX
   What sayst Jugg?

MAID
   The sweetest news.   180

LADY KIX
   What is't wench?

MAID
   Throw down your doctor's drugs,
   They're all but heretics; I bring certain remedy
   That has been taught, and proved, and never failed.

SIR OLIVER
   O that, that, that or nothing.   185

MAID
   There's a gentleman,
   I haply have his name, too, that has got
   Nine children by one water that he useth;
   It never misses, they come so fast upon him,
   He was fain to give it over.

LADY KIX   His name sweet Jugg?   190

MAID
   One Master Touchwood, a fine gentleman,
   But run behind hand much with getting children.

SIR OLIVER
   Is't possible?

---

172 *Bartholomew eve* 23 August; as it is not yet mid-Lent (II.ii.206–7), the children
    were conceived before marriage
179 *Jugg* familiar form of 'Joan', often applied to servants
183 *heretics* Physicians were suspected of using magic.
187 *haply* by chance
188 *water* (a) medicine (b) semen

MAID   Why sir, he'll undertake,
  Using that water, within fifteen year,
  For all your wealth, to make you a poor man,   195
  You shall so swarm with children.
SIR OLIVER
  I'll venture that i'faith.
LADY KIX   That shall you husband.
MAID
  But I must tell you first, he's very dear.
SIR OLIVER
  No matter, what serves wealth for?
LADY KIX   True, sweet husband.
[SIR OLIVER]
  There's land to come; put case his water stands me   200
  In some five hundred pound a pint,
  'Twill fetch a thousand, and a kersten soul.
[LADY KIX]
  And that's worth all, sweet husband.
[SIR OLIVER]
  I'll about it.

                                          Ex[eunt]

[Act II, Scene ii]

Enter ALLWIT

ALLWIT
  I'll go bid gossips presently myself;
  That's all the work I'll do, nor need I stir,
  But that it is my pleasure to walk forth
  And air myself a little; I am tied to nothing
  In this business, what I do is merely recreation,   5
  Not constraint.
  Here's running to and fro, nurse upon nurse,
  Three charwomen, besides maids and neighbours' children.
  Fie, what a trouble have I rid my hands on;
  It makes me sweat to think on't.

---

200 *put case* suppose, with a pun on *case* = vagina
200–204 Q gives all these lines to Lady Kix, reversing the last two. The present
     arrangement follows Parker.
202 *kersten* Christian

  1 *gossips* godparents, but also women friends

Enter SIR WALTER WHOREHOUND

SIR WALTER   How now Jack?   10
ALLWIT
I am going to bid gossips for your worship's child sir;
A goodly girl i'faith, give you joy on her,
She looks as if she had two thousand pound to her portion
And run away with a tailor; a fine plump black eyed slut;
Under correction sir,   15
I take delight to see her: Nurse!

Enter DRY NURSE

DRY NURSE   Do you call sir?
ALLWIT
I call not you, I call the wet nurse hither,

Exit [DRY NURSE]

Give me the wet nurse,

Enter WET NURSE [*carrying baby*]

                              ay, 'tis thou,
Come hither, come hither,
Let's see her once again; I cannot choose   20
But buss her thrice an hour.
WET NURSE
You may be proud on't sir,
'Tis the best piece of work that e'er you did.
ALLWIT
Think'st thou so Nurse? What sayst to Wat and Nick?
WET NURSE
They're pretty children both, but here's a wench   25
Will be a knocker.
ALLWIT
Pup – sayst thou me so? Pup, little countess;
Faith sir I thank your worship for this girl,
Ten thousand times, and upward.
SIR WALTER
I am glad I have her for you sir.   30

---

14 *run away with a tailor* i.e. because she has such fine clothes, but as well, tailors
    were traditionally lecherous; cf. Dekker and Webster, *Northward Ho!*: 'Tailors
    will be saucy and lickerish' (II.i.177)
16 *Nurse* The dry nurse usually looked after the child, the wet nurse suckled it.
21 *buss* kiss
26 *knocker* (a) good-looker (b) notable copulator
27 *countess* A bawdy pun, following 'knocker', but see also note to III.ii.99.

ALLWIT
  Here, take her in Nurse, wipe her, and give her spoon-meat.
WET NURSE
  [*Aside*] Wipe your mouth sir.   *Exit*
ALLWIT
  And now about these gossips.
SIR WALTER
  Get but two, I'll stand for one myself.
ALLWIT
  To your own child sir?   35
SIR WALTER
  The better policy, it prevents suspicion,
  'Tis good to play with rumour at all weapons.
ALLWIT
  Troth, I commend your care sir, 'tis a thing
  That I should ne'er have thought on.
SIR WALTER [*Aside*]   The more slave;
  When man turns base, out goes his soul's pure flame,   40
  The fat of ease o'er-throws the eyes of shame.
ALLWIT
  I am studying who to get for godmother
  Suitable to your worship: now I ha' thought on't.
SIR WALTER
  I'll ease you of that care, and please myself in't.
  [*Aside*] My love the goldsmith's daughter, if I send,   45
  Her father will command her. Davy Dahumma!

                        Enter DAVY

ALLWIT
  I'll fit your worship then with a male partner.
SIR WALTER
  What is he?
ALLWIT
  A kind proper gentleman, brother to Master Touchwood.
SIR WALTER
  I know Touchwood, has he a brother living?   50
ALLWIT
  A neat bachelor.

---

31 *spoon-meat* puréed food for infants
32 *Wipe your mouth* Make a fool of yourself; but this may also refer to 'Such is the
   way of an adulterous woman; she eateth, and wipeth her mouth, and saith, I
   have done no wickedness' (Proverbs 30:20).
51 *neat* elegant

SIR WALTER
Now we know him we'll make shift with him.
Dispatch, the time draws near. Come hither Davy.

                                    Exit [with DAVY]

ALLWIT
In troth I pity him, he ne'er stands still.
Poor knight, what pains he takes – sends this way one,   55
That way another, has not an hour's leisure –
I would not have thy toil, for all thy pleasure.

                Enter TWO PROMOTERS

Ha, how now, what are these that stand so close
At the street corner, pricking up their ears,
And snuffing up their noses, like rich men's dogs   60
When the first course goes in? By the mass, promoters,
'Tis so I hold my life, and planted there
To arrest the dead corps of poor calves and sheep,
Like ravenous creditors that will not suffer
The bodies of their poor departed debtors   65
To go to th' grave, but e'en in death to vex
And stay the corps, with bills of Middlesex.
This Lent will fat the whoresons up with sweetbreads
And lard their whores with lamb-stones; what their golls
Can clutch goes presently to their Molls and Dolls.   70
The bawds will be so fat with what they earn
Their chins will hang like udders by Easter eve,
And being stroked, will give the milk of witches.
How did the mongrels hear my wife lies in?
Well, I may baffle 'em gallantly. By your favour gentlemen,   75
I am a stranger both unto the city

52 *make shift with* be content with
63, 67 *corps* Q has 'corps', an old plural form, but 'corpses' is unmetrical
67 *bills of Middlesex* writs allowing arrests on bogus charges within Middlesex,
    which contained London north of the Thames, so that defendants could be tried
    for crimes committed outside the county
69 *lard . . . lamb-stones* fatten with lambs' testicles, like sweetbreads believed to be
    aphrodisiac
    golls hands (slang)
70 *Molls and Dolls* names used for whores and criminals' girlfriends
72–73 *chins . . . witches* Bawds were believed to be characterized by double chins;
    witches were believed to give suck to the devil, and their familiars, from a third
    nipple somewhere on the body. Middleton also uses this image in *The Black
    Book* (1604). (See Bullen, VIII, 12.)
75 *baffle* insult, treat with indignity

And to her carnal strictness.

1 PROMOTER   Good; your will sir?

ALLWIT
Pray tell me where one dwells that kills this Lent.

1 PROMOTER
How, kills? Come hither Dick,
A bird, a bird.   80

2 PROMOTER
What is't that you would have?

ALLWIT   Faith any flesh,
But I long especially for veal and green sauce.

1 PROMOTER
[Aside] Green goose, you shall be sauced.

ALLWIT
I have half a scornful stomach, no fish will be admitted.

1 PROMOTER
Not this Lent sir?   85

ALLWIT
Lent, what cares colon here for Lent?

1 PROMOTER
You say well sir;
Good reason that the colon of a gentleman,
As you were lately pleased to term your worship sir,
Should be fulfilled with answerable food,   90
To sharpen blood, delight health, and tickle nature.
Were you directed hither to this street sir?

ALLWIT
That I was, ay marry.

2 PROMOTER   And the butcher belike
Should kill and sell close in some upper room?

ALLWIT
Some apple loft as I take it, or a coal house,   95
I know not which i'faith.

2 PROMOTER
Either will serve.

---

80 *bird* victim
82 *green sauce* made with vinegar or verjuice with spices but without garlic; both
   'veal' and 'green' imply gullibility and to eat 'veal and green sauce' = to be cheated
83 *Green goose* (a) young goose made into pies for the goose fair at Bow (b) cant
   term for a cuckold
86 *colon* belly
90 *answerable* suitable
94 *close* secret

[*Aside*] This butcher shall kiss Newgate, 'less he turn up the
Bottom of the pocket of his apron;
You go to seek him?

ALLWIT   Where you shall not find him;   100
I'll buy, walk by your noses with my flesh,
Sheep-biting mongrels, hand basket freebooters!
My wife lies in; a foutra for promoters!   *Exit*

1 PROMOTER
That shall not serve your turn – what a rogue's this; how
cunningly he came over us !   105

Enter a MAN *with meat in a basket*

2 PROMOTER
Husht, stand close.

MAN
I have 'scaped well thus far; they say the knaves are wondrous hot and busy.

1 PROMOTER
By your leave sir,
We must see what you have under your cloak there.   110

MAN
Have? I have nothing.

1 PROMOTER
No, do you tell us that? What makes this lump stick out
then; we must see sir.

MAN
What will you see sir – a pair of sheets, and two of my
wife's foul smocks, going to the washers?   115

2 PROMOTER
O we love that sight well, you cannot please us better:
what, do you gull us? Call you these shirts and smocks?

MAN
Now a pox choke you!
You have cozened me and five of my wife's kindred
Of a good dinner; we must make it up now   120

---

98 *kiss Newgate* go to prison; one of the gates of ancient London, Newgate was used as
     a prison for the worst class of criminals from at least 1190; it was demolished 1902–3

98–9 *turn . . . apron* offer a bribe

102 *sheep-biting* whoring
      freebooters pirates, here raiding the baskets of passers-by; perhaps with a pun on
      basket = whore

103 *foutra* vulgarism for the sexual act; from the French 'foutre'

104 *serve your turn* (a) 'Your wife's pregnancy can't be used as an excuse'; under the stricter
      laws of 1613 it was illegal even for invalids and pregnant women to eat meat in Lent
      (b) continuing the sense of 'foutra', since one turns the body to be served sexually

With herrings and milk pottage.   *Exit*

1 PROMOTER
'Tis all veal.

2 PROMOTER
All veal? Pox the worse luck; I promised faithfully to send
this morning a fat quarter of lamb to a kind gentlewoman
in Turnbull street that longs, and how I'm crossed.   125

1 PROMOTER
Let's share this, and see what hap comes next then.

Enter another [MAN] *with a basket*

2 PROMOTER
Agreed, stand close again; another booty.
What's he?

1 PROMOTER
Sir, by your favour.

2 MAN
Meaning me sir?   130

1 PROMOTER
Good Master Oliver, cry thee mercy, i'faith.
What hast thou there?

2 MAN
A rack of mutton sir, and half a lamb;
You know my mistress's diet.

1 PROMOTER
Go, go, we see thee not; away, keep close.   135
Heart, let him pass, thou'lt never have the wit
To know our benefactors.

                                             [*Exit* MAN]

2 PROMOTER
I have forgot him.

1 PROMOTER
'Tis Master Beggarland's man, the wealthy merchant
That is in fee with us.   140

2 PROMOTER
Now I have a feeling of him.

---

121 *pottage* broth
125 *Turnbull Street* (corrupted form of Turnmill) ran between Clerkenwell Green
     and Cowcross Street, and was the most notorious street in London for its thieves
     and whores, one of whom *longs* because she is pregnant
133 *rack* neck

1 PROMOTER
You know he purchased the whole Lent together,
Gave us ten groats apiece on Ash Wednesday.
2 PROMOTER
True, true.

Enter a WENCH *with a basket, and a child in it under a*
loin of mutton

1 PROMOTER
A wench.   145
2 PROMOTER
Why then stand close indeed.
WENCH
[*Aside*] Women had need of wit, if they'll shift here,
And she that hath wit may shift anywhere.
1 PROMOTER
Look, look, poor fool,
She has left the rump uncovered too,   150
More to betray her; this is like a murderer
That will outface the deed with a bloody band.
2 PROMOTER
What time of the year is't sister?
WENCH
O sweet gentlemen, I am a poor servant,
Let me go.   155
1 PROMOTER
You shall wench, but this must stay with us.
WENCH
O you undo me sir;
'Tis for a wealthy gentlewoman that takes physic sir,
The doctor does allow my mistress mutton,
O as you tender the dear life of a gentlewoman,   160
I'll bring my master to you, he shall show you

142 *purchased the whole Lent together* paid them for immunity over the 40 days of
      Lent, which began on Ash Wednesday
143 *groats* first coined 1351–2, made equal to fourpence; by 1600 used for any small
      sum
144 s.d. The trick played by the country wench is also found in some ballads, e.g.
      'The Country Girl's Policy, or the Cockney Outwitted' and 'A Tryall of Skill,
      performed by a poor decay'd Gentlewoman' (*Roxburghe Ballads*, ed. J. W.
      Ebsworth (1880–1890), VII, 286 and IX, 556).
147 *wit* (a) cleverness (b) cunt. Cf. Middleton, *More Dissemblers Besides Women*
      IV.ii.230–5, Shakespeare, *As You Like It* IV.i.155.
      shift (a) succeed (b) live by fraud (c) palm off something on someone
152 *band* collar; standing collars were popular 1605–30. Possibly a wristband.

A true authority from the higher powers,
And I'll run every foot.

2 PROMOTER
Well, leave your basket then,
And run and spare not.   165

WENCH
Will you swear then to me
To keep it till I come.

1 PROMOTER
Now by this light I will.

WENCH
What say you, gentleman?

2 PROMOTER
What a strange wench 'tis.   170
Would we might perish else.

WENCH
Nay then I run sir.   *Exit*

1 PROMOTER
And ne'er return I hope.

2 PROMOTER
A politic baggage,
She makes us swear to keep it;   175
I prithee look what market she hath made.

1 PROMOTER
Imprimis sir, a good fat loin of mutton;
What comes next under this cloth?
Now for a quarter of lamb.

2 PROMOTER
Now for a shoulder of mutton.   180

1 PROMOTER
Done.

2 PROMOTER
Why done sir?

1 PROMOTER
By the mass I feel I have lost,
'Tis of more weight i'faith.

2 PROMOTER
Some loin of veal?   185

1 PROMOTER
No faith, here's a lamb's head,

---

162 *true authority* The sick, and some foreign ambassadors, were permitted by the
   city authorities to have meat during Lent.
174 *politic* cunning
177 *Imprimis* 'In the first place'
180 *Now* ed. (not Q)

I feel that plainly, why yet I'll win my wager.

2 PROMOTER
Ha?

1 PROMOTER
Swounds what's here?

2 PROMOTER
A child.   190

1 PROMOTER
A pox of all dissembling cunning whores.

2 PROMOTER
Here's an unlucky breakfast.

1 PROMOTER
What shall's do?

2 PROMOTER
The quean made us swear to keep it too.

1 PROMOTER
We might leave it else.   195

2 PROMOTER
Villainous strange;
Life, had she none to gull but poor promoters
That watch hard for a living?

1 PROMOTER
Half our gettings must run in sugar-sops
And nurses' wages now, besides many a pound of soap,   200
And tallow; we have need to get loins of mutton still,
To save suet to change for candles.

2 PROMOTER
Nothing mads me but this was a lamb's head with you, you
felt it; she has made calves' heads of us.

1 PROMOTER
Prithee no more on't,   205
There's time to get it up; it is not come
To mid-Lent Sunday yet.

2 PROMOTER
I am so angry, I'll watch no more today.

1 PROMOTER
Faith nor I neither.

187 *I'll* ed. (Q omits)
189 *Swounds* 'God's wounds'
194 *quean* whore
199 *sugar-sops* bread soaked in sugar water
201 *tallow* used for candles and also perhaps for babies' bottoms
203–4 *Nothing . . . us* 'Nothing makes me so annoyed as to think that you, who felt
       the baby, said it was a lamb's head; she's made fools of us'
206 *get it up* make up the money we've lost

2 PROMOTER
  Why then I'll make a motion.   210
1 PROMOTER
  Well, what is't?
2 PROMOTER
  Let's e'en go to the Checker at Queen-hive and roast the
  loin of mutton, till young flood; then send the child to
  Branford.

                                                        [*Exeunt*]

                      [Act II, Scene iii]

              Enter ALLWIT *in one of Sir Walter's suits, and*
                          DAVY *trussing him*

ALLWIT
  'Tis a busy day at our house Davy.
DAVY
  Always the kursning day sir.
ALLWIT
  Truss, truss me Davy.
DAVY
  [*Aside*] No matter and you were hanged sir.
ALLWIT
  How does this suit fit me Davy?   5
DAVY
  Excellent neatly; my master's things were ever fit for you
  sir, e'en to a hair you know.

212 *Checker* an inn, with a chess-board as its sign, which gave its name to the lane
     where it stood (cf. *Survey*, I, 231)
     Queen-hive Queenhithe, 'the very chief and principal water-gate of this city'
     (*Survey*, I, 41), a quay on the north bank of the Thames
213 *young flood* the beginning of the rising tide
214 *Branford* Brentford, eight miles upstream from London and a resort of whores
     as well as other citizens, usually spelt 'Brainford', as at V.iv.97

  0 s.d. *trussing* tying the points of his hose to his doublet; 'to truss' also means 'to
         hang'
  2 *kursning day* christening day
  4 *No matter and* It wouldn't matter if
  6 *things* (a) clothes (b) sexual organs (in this case Mrs Allwit's)
  7 *e'en to a hair* (a) exactly (b) right up to the pubic hair (c) even to begetting an
    heir

ALLWIT
Thou has hit it right Davy,
We ever jumped in one, this ten years Davy.

Enter a SERVANT *with a box*

So, well said. What art thou?   10
SERVANT
Your comfit-maker's man sir.
ALLWIT
 O sweet youth, into the nurse quick,
Quick, 'tis time i'faith;
Your mistress will be here?
SERVANT
She was setting forth sir.   15

Enter TWO PURITANS

ALLWIT
Here comes our gossips now, O I shall have such kissing
work today; sweet Mistress Underman welcome i'faith.
I PURITAN
Give you joy of your fine girl sir,
Grant that her education may be pure,
And become one of the faithful.   20
ALLWIT
Thanks to your sisterly wishes Mistress Underman.
2 PURITAN
Are any of the brethren's wives yet come?
ALLWIT
There are some wives within, and some at home.
I PURITAN
Verily thanks sir.

Ex[eunt PURITANS]

ALLWIT
Verily you are an ass forsooth;   25
I must fit all these times, or there's no music.

---

9 *jumped in one* (a) agreed (b) copulated with the same woman. Either Allwit has been
  deceiving Sir Walter, despite his protestation at I.ii.107, or he's joking. Cf. V.i.167.
10 *well said* well done. This expression occurs several times in the play.
11 *comfit* sweet made by mixing the pulp of cooked fruit with sugar
26 'I have to be agreeable with all these people or else there'll be no kissing'; cf.
  Dekker and Webster, *Westward Ho!* V.iv.283, 'Every husband play music upon
  the lips of his wife'. Allwit is out to enjoy himself.
  times rhythms

Enter TWO GOSSIPS

Here comes a friendly and familiar pair –
Now I like these wenches well.

1 GOSSIP
How dost sirrah?

ALLWIT
Faith well I thank you neighbour, and how dost thou?   30

2 GOSSIP
Want nothing, but such getting sir as thine.

ALLWIT
My gettings wench, they are poor.

1 GOSSIP
Fie that thou'lt say so,
Th'ast as fine children as a man can get.

DAVY
[*Aside*] Ay, as a man can get,   35
And that's my master.

ALLWIT
They are pretty foolish things,
Put to making in minutes;
I ne'er stand long about 'em,
Will you walk in wenches?   40

[*Exeunt* GOSSIPS]

Enter TOUCHWOOD JUNIOR *and* MOLL

TOUCHWOOD JUNIOR
The happiest meeting that our souls could wish for. Here's
the ring ready; I am beholding unto your father's haste, h'as
kept his hour.

MOLL
He never kept it better.

Enter SIR WALTER WHOREHOUND [*with a goblet*]

TOUCHWOOD JUNIOR
Back, be silent.   45

SIR WALTER
Mistress and partner, I will put you both into one cup.

[*Drinks*]

DAVY
Into one cup, most proper,

---

32 *gettings* (a) begettings (b) earnings
42 *beholding* beholden
47 *into one cup* pledge them both in one drink – a nice irony, since at a betrothal
ceremony the betrothed couple would drink from the same loving cup

A fitting compliment for a goldsmith's daughter.

ALLWIT
Yes sir, that's he must be your worship's partner
In this day's business, Master Touchwood's brother.   50

SIR WALTER
I embrace your acquaintance sir.

TOUCHWOOD JUNIOR
It vows your service sir.

SIR WALTER
It's near high time, come Master Allwit.

ALLWIT
Ready sir.

SIR WALTER
Will't please you walk?   55

TOUCHWOOD JUNIOR
Sir I obey your time.

                                                     Ex[eunt]

         Enter MIDWIFE with the child, [MAUDLINE] and the
                    GOSSIPS to the kursning

I GOSSIP
Good Mistress Yellowhammer.

MAUDLINE
In faith I will not.

I GOSSIP
Indeed it shall be yours.

MAUDLINE
I have sworn i'faith.   60

I GOSSIP
I'll stand still then.

MAUDLINE
So will you let the child go without company
And make me forsworn.

I GOSSIP
You are such another creature.

                              [Exeunt I GOSSIP and MAUDLINE]

2 GOSSIP
Before me? I pray come down a little.   65

53 *near high time* nearly noon. Cf. 'this morning' II.ii.124.
56 *time* beat (continuing the musical imagery of l. 26)
56 s.d. During this progress across the stage, the women are squabbling over prece-
     dence in following the child into the room.

3 GOSSIP
  Not a whit; I hope I know my place.
2 GOSSIP
  Your place? Great wonder sure! Are you any better than a
  comfit-maker's wife?
3 GOSSIP
  And that's as good at all times as a 'pothecary's.
2 GOSSIP
  Ye lie, yet I forbear you too.   70

                    [*Exeunt* 2 *and* 3 GOSSIPS]

1 PURITAN
  Come sweet sister, we go in unity, and show the fruits of
  peace like children of the spirit.
2 PURITAN
  I love lowliness.
4 GOSSIP
  True, so say I, though they strive more,
  There comes as proud behind, as goes before.   75
5 GOSSIP
  Every inch, i'faith.

                                                    Ex[*eunt*]

Act III, [Scene i]

Enter TOUCHWOOD JUNIOR *and a* PARSON

TOUCHWOOD JUNIOR
  O sir, if ever you felt the force of love, pity it in me.
PARSON
  Yes, though I ne'er was married sir,
  I have felt the force of love from good men's daughters,
  And some that will be maids yet three years hence.
  Have you got a licence?   5
TOUCHWOOD JUNIOR
  Here 'tis ready sir.
PARSON
  That's well.

---

  75 *There comes as proud* . . . Proverbial, but the meaning of 'proud' as sexually
     excited is taken up in the next line.

  2–5 The parson implies a sexual past. Cf. II.i.70–72.
  5 *licence* See note to II.i.128.

TOUCHWOOD JUNIOR
    The ring and all things perfect; she'll steal hither.
PARSON
    She shall be welcome sir; I'll not be long
    A-clapping you together.

        Enter MOLL *and* TOUCHWOOD SENIOR

TOUCHWOOD JUNIOR   O here she's come sir.   10
PARSON
    What's he?
TOUCHWOOD JUNIOR My honest brother.
TOUCHWOOD SENIOR   Quick, make haste sirs.
MOLL
    You must dispatch with all the speed you can,
    For I shall be missed straight; I made hard shift
    For this small time I have.
PARSON   Then I'll not linger:
    Place that ring upon her finger,   15
    This the finger plays the part,
    Whose master vein shoots from the heart;
    Now join hands.

        Enter YELLOWHAMMER *and* SIR WALTER

YELLOWHAMMER   Which I will sever;
    And so ne'er again meet never.
MOLL
    O we are betrayed.
TOUCHWOOD JUNIOR Hard fate.
SIR WALTER   I am struck with wonder.   20
YELLOWHAMMER
    Was this the politic fetch, thou mystical baggage,
    Thou disobedient strumpet?
    And were so wise to send for her to such an end?
SIR WALTER
    Now I disclaim the end, you'll make me mad.

---

17 *heart* Popular superstition had it that a vein or nerve ran from the third finger of
    the left hand to the heart; cf. note to I.ii.55–6
18 *join hands* A marriage contract was made legal by 'handfasting', the joining of
    hands. Cf. Polixenes' similar intervention preventing the marriage of his son
    Florizel to Perdita in *The Winter's Tale* IV.iv.417.
21 *politic fetch* cunning trick, stratagem
    thou used instead of 'you' to indicate Yellowhammer's anger and contempt for
    his daughter
    mystical secret

YELLOWHAMMER
  And what are you sir?   25
TOUCHWOOD JUNIOR
  And you cannot see with those two glasses, put on a pair
  more.
YELLOWHAMMER
  I dreamt of anger still – here take your ring sir;
  Ha this? Life 'tis the same: abominable!
  Did not I sell this ring?   30
TOUCHWOOD JUNIOR
  I think you did, you received money for it.
YELLOWHAMMER
  Heart, hark you knight,
  Here's no inconscionable villainy –
  Set me a-work to make the wedding ring,
  And come with an intent to steal my daughter;   35
  Did ever runaway match it?
SIR WALTER
  This your brother sir?
TOUCHWOOD SENIOR
  He can tell that as well as I.
YELLOWHAMMER
  The very posy mocks me to my face:
  'Love that's wise, blinds parents' eyes.'   40
  I thank your wisdom sir for blinding of us;
  We have good hope to recover our sight shortly;
  In the meantime I will lock up this baggage
  As carefully as my gold; she shall see as little sun,
  If a close room or so can keep her from the light on't.   45
MOLL
  O sweet father, for love's sake pity me.
YELLOWHAMMER
  Away!
MOLL
  Farewell sir, all content bless thee,
  And take this for comfort,
  Though violence keep me, thou canst lose me never,   50
  I am ever thine although we part for ever.
YELLOWHAMMER
  Ay, we shall part you minx.

Exit [YELLOWHAMMER *with* MOLL]

---

26 *glasses* his eyes, or perhaps spectacles
28 *still* always; 'I always only dreamed of being angry, now I am'
43–5 Cf. Corvino's treatment of his wife Celia in Jonson's *Volpone* II.v.

SIR WALTER
  Your acquaintance sir came very lately,
  Yet it came too soon;
  I must hereafter know you for no friend,   55
  But one that I must shun like pestilence,
  Or the disease of lust.
TOUCHWOOD JUNIOR
  Like enough sir, you ha' ta'en me at the worst time for
  words that e'er ye picked out; faith do not wrong me sir.
                                                      Exit

TOUCHWOOD SENIOR
  Look after him and spare not; there he walks   60
  That never yet received baffling; you're blessed
  More than e'er I knew. Go take your rest.   *Exit*
SIR WALTER
  I pardon you, you are both losers.   *Exit*

[Act III, Scene ii]

A bed thrust out upon the stage, ALLWIT'S WIFE *in it.*
Enter all the GOSSIPS *[including* MAUDLINE *and*
LADY KIX]

I GOSSIP
  How is't woman? We have brought you home
  A kursen soul.
MISTRESS ALLWIT
  Ay, I thank your pains.
I PURITAN
  And verily well kursened, i'the right way,
  Without idolatry or superstition,   5

60 *Look after him* Beware of him
61 *baffling* insult, public humiliation

0 s.d. *A bed* Cf. R. Brome and T. Heywood, *The Late Lancashire Witches* (1634),
   Act V, '*A Bed thrust out, Mrs Gener[ous] in't*'. Richard Hosley found 23
   instances of staging a bed in Chamberlain's / King's Men plays 1595–62; in 8 it
   is stated, and in 8 others implied, that the bed was brought on stage (see
   Shakespeare Quarterly 14 (1963), 57–63). This could have been done by stage
   attendants, but in the Adelaide Theatre Group production (1971) Mrs Allwit's
   bed was pushed on, very rapidly, by other cast members.
2 *kursen* Christian, but with a pun on 'cursed', as the christening was 'After the
   pure manner of Amsterdam', and therefore thoroughly Puritan

After the pure manner of Amsterdam.

MISTRESS ALLWIT
Sit down good neighbours; Nurse!

NURSE
At hand forsooth.

MISTRESS ALLWIT
Look they have all low stools.

NURSE
They have forsooth.   10

2 GOSSIP
Bring the child hither Nurse; how say you now
Gossip, is't not a chopping girl, so like the father?

3 GOSSIP
As if it had been spit out of his mouth,
Eyed, nosed and browed as like a girl can be,
Only indeed it has the mother's mouth.   15

2 GOSSIP
The mother's mouth up and down, up and down.

3 GOSSIP
'Tis a large child, she's but a little woman.

1 PURITAN
No believe me, a very spiny creature, but all heart,
Well mettled, like the faithful to endure
Her tribulation here, and raise up seed.   20

2 GOSSIP
She had a sore labour on't I warrant you, you can tell
neighbour.

3 GOSSIP
O she had great speed;
We were afraid once,
But she made us all have joyful hearts again;   25
'Tis a good soul i'faith;
The midwife found her a most cheerful daughter.

1 PURITAN
'Tis the spirit, the sisters are all like her.

6 *Amsterdam* meeting place and refuge for European dissenters, symbolic of
  Puritanism

12 *chopping* vigorous, strapping

13 *spit out of his mouth* proverbial

16 *up and down* (a) exactly (b) oral and vaginal; cf. the song, IV.i.187

18 *spiny* thin, spare

19 *mettled* courageous, with a pun on the meaning 'amorous'

Enter SIR WALTER *with two spoons and plate, and*
ALLWIT

2 GOSSIP
O here comes the chief gossip neighbours.

SIR WALTER
The fatness of your wishes to you all ladies.   30

3 GOSSIP
O dear sweet gentleman, what fine words he has –
'The fatness of our wishes'!

2 GOSSIP
Calls us all 'ladies'!

4 GOSSIP
I promise you, a fine gentleman, and a courteous.

2 GOSSIP
Methinks her husband shows like a clown to him.   35

3 GOSSIP
I would not care what clown my husband were too, so I
had such fine children.

2 GOSSIP
She's all fine children gossip.

3 GOSSIP
Ay, and see how fast they come.

I PURITAN
Children are blessings, if they be got with zeal   40
By the brethren, as I have five at home.

SIR WALTER
The worst is past, I hope now gossip.

MISTRESS ALLWIT
So I hope too good sir.

ALLWIT
Why then so hope I too for company,
I have nothing to do else.   45

SIR WALTER
A poor remembrance lady,
To the love of the babe; I pray accept of it.

MISTRESS ALLWIT
O you are at too much charge sir.

2 GOSSIP
Look, look, what has he given her, what is't gossip?

---

28 s.d. *plate* gold or silver ware
35 *clown* country bumpkin
38 *She's* She has
40 *zeal* religious zeal, but also sexual enthusiasm (cf. I.i.148)

3 GOSSIP
Now by my faith a fair high standing cup, and two great   50
'postle spoons, one of them gilt.

1 PURITAN
Sure that was Judas then with the red beard.

2 PURITAN
I would not feed my daughter with that spoon for all the
world, for fear of colouring her hair; red hair the brethren
like not, it consumes them much, 'tis not the sisters' colour.   55

Enter NURSE *with comfits and wine*

ALLWIT
Well said Nurse;
About, about with them amongst the gossips:
Now out comes all the tasseled handkerchers,
They are spread abroad between their knees already;
Now in goes the long fingers that are washed   60
Some thrice a day in urine – my wife uses it –
Now we shall have such pocketing;
See how they lurch at the lower end.

1 PURITAN
Come hither Nurse.

ALLWIT
Again! She has taken twice already.   65

1 PURITAN
I had forgot a sister's child that's sick.

ALLWIT
A pox, it seems your purity loves sweet things well that puts
in thrice together. Had this been all my cost now I had been
beggared. These women have no consciences at sweet-

---

50 *high standing cup* stemmed goblet
51 *'postle spoons* usually silver, the handles ending in the figure of an apostle, often
   given by sponsors at christenings
   gilt silver covered with gold
52 *Judas . . . red beard* Ancient belief; Judas wore a red beard in medieval religious
   drama. The supposition that red hair denoted lechery (cf. the Welsh
   Gentlewoman) as well as evil generally persisted in the theatre into the late nine-
   teenth century, so that villains sometimes wore red wigs.
55 *consumes* (a) burns (in anger) (b) consummates sexually
58 *tasseled* Handkerchiefs were fashionably large, ornamental and had tassels at the
   corners.
61 *urine* was used as a cosmetic lotion, including as a dentifrice
63 *lurch at the lower end* eat up the food as quickly as possible to prevent those at
   the other end of the room from getting much (or any); but with a possible bawdy
   pun on *lower end*

meats, where e'er they come; see and they have not culled   70
out all the long plums too – they have left nothing here but
short wriggle-tail comfits, not worth mouthing; no mar'l I
heard a citizen complain once that his wife's belly only
broke his back: mine had been all in fitters seven years
since, but for this worthy knight that with a prop upholds   75
my wife and me, and all my estate buried in Bucklersbury.

MISTRESS ALLWIT
Here Mistress Yellowhammer, and neighbours,
To you all that have taken pains with me,
All the good wives at once.

1 PURITAN
I'll answer for them;   80
They wish all health and strength,
And that you may courageously go forward,
To perform the like and many such,
Like a true sister with motherly bearing.

ALLWIT
Now the cups troll about to wet the gossips' whistles;   85
It pours down i'faith: they never think of payment.

1 PURITAN
Fill again nurse.

ALLWIT
Now bless thee, two at once; I'll stay no longer;
It would kill me and if I paid for't.
Will it please you to walk down and leave the women?   90

SIR WALTER
With all my heart Jack.

ALLWIT
Troth I cannot blame you.

SIR WALTER
Sit you all merry ladies.

ALL GOSSIPS
Thank your worship sir.

71 *plums* sugar plums
72 *wriggle-tail* tiny
73–4 *belly only broke his back* (a) her greed alone made him overwork and (b) her
      lust left him exhausted
74 *fitters* fragments
76 *Bucklersbury* runs south from the corner of Cheapside and the Poultry to
      Walbrook; 'on both the sides throughout [it was] possessed of grocers and
      apothecaries' (*Survey*, I, 260); Allwit is saying the catering for all the christen-
      ings of his wife's children over the years would have ruined him
85 *troll* pass about
93 *merry* (a) happy (b) tipsy

1 PURITAN
Thank your worship sir.   95
ALLWIT
A pox twice tipple ye, you are last and lowest.

                        Exit [ALLWIT *with* SIR WALTER]

1 PURITAN
Bring hither that same cup Nurse, I would fain drive away
this – hup! – antichristian grief.

                        [NURSE *refills goblet, then exits*]

3 GOSSIP
See gossip and she lies not in like a countess;
Would I had such a husband for my daughter.   100
4 GOSSIP
Is not she toward marriage?
3 GOSSIP
O no sweet gossip.
4 GOSSIP
Why, she's nineteen?
3 GOSSIP
Ay that she was last Lammas,
But she has a fault gossip, a secret fault.   105
4 GOSSIP
A fault, what is't?
3 GOSSIP
I'll tell you when I have drunk.
4 GOSSIP
Wine can do that, I see, that friendship cannot.
3 GOSSIP
And now I'll tell you gossip – she's too free.
4 GOSSIP
Too free?   110
3 GOSSIP
O ay, she cannot lie dry in her bed.
4 GOSSIP
What, and nineteen?

---

96 *tipple* tumble
99 *countess* At the end of January 1613 it was reported that 'the Countess of
   Salisbury was brought abed of a daughter, and lies in very richly, for the hanging of her chamber, being white satin, embroidered with gold (or silver) and
   pearl is valued at fourteen thousand pounds' (John Chamberlain, *Letters*, ed. N.
   E. McLure (Philadelphia, 1939), I, 415–16).
104 *Lammas* 1 August; harvest festival of the early English church

3 GOSSIP
'Tis as I tell you gossip.

[*Enter* NURSE *and speaks to* MAUDLINE]

MAUDLINE
Speak with me Nurse? Who is't?
NURSE
A gentleman from Cambridge,   115
I think it be your son forsooth.
MAUDLINE
'Tis my son Tim i'faith,
Prithee call him up among the women,

[*Exit* NURSE]

'Twill embolden him well,
For he wants nothing but audacity;   120
Would the Welsh gentlewoman at home were here now.
LADY KIX
Is your son come forsooth?
MAUDLINE
Yes from the university forsooth.
LADY KIX
'Tis a great joy on ye.
MAUDLINE
There's a great marriage towards for him.   125
LADY KIX
A marriage?
MAUDLINE
Yes sure, a huge heir in Wales,
At least to nineteen mountains,
Besides her goods and cattle.

Enter TIM [*and* NURSE]

TIM
O, I'm betrayed.   *Exit*   130
MAUDLINE
What gone again? Run after him good Nurse;

[*Exit* NURSE]

He's so bashful, that's the spoil of youth;
In the university they're kept still to men,

---

129 *cattle* property (as in 'chattels', another form of the word), including in this case
the Welshwoman's 'Two thousand runts' (IV.i.94)
133 *still* always

And ne'er trained up to women's company.

LADY KIX
'Tis a great spoil of youth, indeed.   135

Enter NURSE *and* TIM

NURSE
Your mother will have it so.

MAUDLINE
Why son, why Tim; what, must I rise and fetch you? For
shame son.

TIM
Mother you do intreat like a freshwoman;
'Tis against the laws of the university   140
For any that has answered under bachelor
To thrust 'mongst married wives.

MAUDLINE
Come we'll excuse you here.

TIM
Call up my tutor mother, and I care not.

MAUDLINE
What, is your tutor come? Have you brought him up?   145

TIM
I ha' not brought him up, he stands at door,
Negatur, there's logic to begin with you mother.

MAUDLINE
Run call the gentleman Nurse, he's my son's tutor;
Here eat some plums.

                                                    [*Exit* NURSE]

TIM
Come I from Cambridge, and offer me six plums?   150

MAUDLINE
Why how now Tim,
Will not your old tricks yet be left?

TIM
Served like a child,
When I have answered under bachelor?

---

139 *freshwoman* Tim's nonce word from 'freshman', a first-year university student.
     Cambridge University did not admit women to full membership, awarding them
     degrees, until 1947, though the first women's college, Girton, had been founded
     in 1869.

141 *answered under bachelor* satisfied the requirements for a Bachelor's degree

147 *Negatur* 'It is denied'; standard Latin phrase in academic disputation

MAUDLINE
    You'll never lin till I make your tutor whip you; you know   155
    how I served you once at the free school in Paul's church-
    yard?
TIM
    O monstrous absurdity!
    Ne'er was the like in Cambridge since my time;
    Life, whip a bachelor? You'd be laughed at soundly;   160
    Let not my tutor hear you,
    'Twould be a jest through the whole university;
    No more words mother.

                        Enter TUTOR

MAUDLINE
    Is this your tutor Tim?
TUTOR
    Yes surely lady, I am the man that brought him in league   165
    with logic, and read the Dunces to him.
TIM
    That did he mother, but now I have 'em all in my own pate,
    and can as well read 'em to others.
TUTOR
    That can he mistress, for they flow naturally from him.
MAUDLINE
    I'm the more beholding to your pains sir.   170
TUTOR
    Non ideo sane.
MAUDLINE   True, he was an idiot indeed
    When he went out of London, but now he's well mended;
    Did you receive the two goose pies I sent you?
TUTOR
    And eat them heartily, thanks to your worship.

155 *lin* cease
     whip To be whipped as a disciplinary measure was a great disgrace.
156 *free school* St Paul's school was rebuilt and largely endowed in 1512 by John
     Colet, Dean of Paul's, for 153 poor scholars; William Lily was the first high
     master, but Tim may have been there under the illustrious Richard Mulcaster
     (1596–1608).
166 *Dunces* (a) writings of Duns Scotus (1265?–1308?) and supporters of his theo-
     logical views, which were attacked by the humanists and reformers of the 16th
     century (b) fools
169 *naturally* (a) spontaneously (b) foolishly
171 *Non ideo sane* 'Not indeed on that account'
173 *goose pies* made with a jointed goose, spices, ale, fried onions and wine, baked
     in pastry; here the word accentuates Tim's foolishness

MAUDLINE
  'Tis my son Tim, I pray bid him welcome gentlewomen.   175
TIM
  'Tim'? Hark you, 'Timothius' mother, 'Timothius'!
MAUDLINE
  How, shall I deny your name? 'Timothius', quoth he?
  Faith there's a name, 'tis my son Tim forsooth.
LADY KIX
  You're welcome Master Tim.   *Kiss*
TIM
  O this is horrible, she wets as she kisses;   180
  Your handkercher sweet tutor, to wipe them off, as fast as
  they come on.
2 GOSSIP
  Welcome from Cambridge.   *Kiss*
TIM
  This is intolerable! This woman has a villainous sweet
  breath, did she not stink of comfits; help me sweet tutor, or   185
  I shall rub my lips off.
TUTOR
  I'll go kiss the lower end the whilst.
TIM
  Perhaps that's the sweeter, and we shall dispatch the
  sooner.
1 PURITAN
  Let me come next. Welcome from the wellspring of disci-   190
  pline, that waters all the brethren.   *Reels and falls*
TIM
  Hoist, I beseech thee.
3 GOSSIP
  O bless the woman – Mistress Underman!
1 PURITAN
  'Tis but the common affliction of the faithful,
  We must embrace our falls.   195
TIM
  I'm glad I 'scaped it, it was some rotten kiss sure,

---

176 *Timothius* The correct Latin is *Timotheus* = 'Honouring God'.
179 s.d. *Kiss* The English were at this time notorious for the freedom with which they
    kissed in greeting.
185 *comfits* 'kissing-comfits' were intended to sweeten the breath
190–91 *Welcome . . . brethren* Cambridge was the intellectual centre of Puritanism
    and its closeness to the Continent made it more accessible than Oxford to
    Calvinist influence.
195 *embrace our falls* An opportunistic and over-literal interpretation of Calvin's
    doctrine that humankind's fallen state must be humbly accepted.

It dropped down before it came at me.

Enter ALLWIT *and* DAVY

ALLWIT
  Here's a noise! Not parted yet?
  Hyda, a looking glass; they have drunk so hard in plate,
  That some of them had need of other vessels.   200
  Yonder's the bravest show.
ALL GOSSIPS
  Where? Where sir?
ALLWIT
  Come along presently by the Pissing-conduit,
  With two brave drums and a standard bearer.
ALL GOSSIPS
  O brave.   205
TIM
  Come tutor.

                                        Ex[eunt TIM *and* TUTOR]

ALL GOSSIPS
  Farewell sweet gossip.

                                        Ex[eunt GOSSIPS]

MISTRESS ALLWIT
  I thank you all for your pains.
I PURITAN
  Feed and grow strong.   *Exit*
ALLWIT
  You had more need to sleep than eat;   210

198 *parted* departed
199 *looking glass* (a) Mistress Underman is still on the floor and the sarcastic Allwit
     calls for a looking glass to see if she is still breathing; cf. *King Lear* V.iii.262–5
     (b) a chamber pot
201 *show* procession
203 *Pissing-conduit* Possibly the conduit at the western end of Cheapside, near Paul's
     Gate and Bladder Street, named here from the slenderness of its stream of water.
     The name could be both generic and specific. The 'little Conduit, called the piss-
     ing Conduit' by Stow (I, 183) was by the Stocks Market, beyond Poultry, and so
     not in Cheapside itself, though Parker and Barber both prefer this to the Paul's
     Gate conduit. See E. H. Sugden, *A Topographical Dictionary to the Works of
     Shakespeare and his Fellow Dramatists* (Manchester, 1925), p. 127.
204 *two . . . drums and a standard bearer* The phallic symbolism, which so excites
     the gossips, is obvious.

Go take a nap with some of the brethren, go,
And rise up a well edified, boldified sister;
O here's a day of toil well passed o'er,
Able to make a citizen hare-mad;
How hot they have made the room with their thick bums;   215
Dost not feel it Davy?

DAVY

Monstrous strong sir.

ALLWIT

What's here under the stools?

DAVY

Nothing but wet sir, some wine spilt here belike.

ALLWIT

Is't no worse thinkst thou?   220
Fair needlework stools cost nothing with them Davy.

DAVY

[Aside] Nor you neither i'faith.

ALLWIT

Look how they have laid them,
E'en as they lie themselves, with their heels up;
How they have shuffled up the rushes too Davy,   225
With their short figging little shittle-cork heels;
These women can let nothing stand as they find it;
But what's the secret thou'st about to tell me
My honest Davy?

DAVY

If you should disclose it sir –   230

ALLWIT

Life, rip my belly up to the throat then Davy.

211 *nap* Anabaptists held that a man and a woman could lie together without moral taint provided they were asleep.

214 *hare-mad* Hares grow wilder in the breeding season, around March.

215 *bums* (a) padded rolls worn on the hips beneath the skirt (b) backsides

218 *stools* Padded furniture was becoming fashionable, large sums being spent on embroidered coverings.

225 *rushes* An indication that rushes were strewn on the public theatre stage, as well as on the floors of houses.

226 *figging* fucking, but a generally derisive term used here in a line of concentrated bawdiness
    short . . . heels 'short-heeled' = wanton; cf. *Revenger's Tragedy* I.ii.184, 'Their tongues as short and nimble as their heels'
    shittle-cork wedge heels (and soles) of cork, fashionable 1595–1620; 'shittle' = shuttle as in 'shuttle-cock' (which was slang for 'whore')

231 *Life* 'God's life'

DAVY
  My master's upon marriage.
ALLWIT
  Marriage Davy? Send me to hanging rather.
DAVY
  [*Aside*] I have stung him.
ALLWIT
  When, where? What is she Davy?   235
DAVY
  E'en the same was gossip, and gave the spoon.
ALLWIT
  I have no time to stay, nor scarce can speak,
  I'll stop those wheels, or all the work will break.   *Exit*
DAVY
  I knew 'twould prick. Thus do I fashion still
  All mine own ends by him and his rank toil;   240
  'Tis my desire to keep him still from marriage;
  Being his poor nearest kinsman, I may fare
  The better at his death; there my hopes build
  Since my Lady Kix is dry, and hath no child.   *Exit*

[Act III, Scene iii]

Enter both the TOUCHWOODS

TOUCHWOOD JUNIOR
  Y'are in the happiest way to enrich yourself,
  And pleasure me brother, as man's feet can tread in,
  For though she be locked up, her vow is fixed only to me;
  Then time shall never grieve me, for by that vow,
  E'en absent I enjoy her, assuredly confirmed that none   5
  Else shall, which will make tedious years seem gameful
  To me. In the mean space lose you no time sweet brother;
  You have the means to strike at this knight's fortunes
  And lay him level with his bankrupt merit;

237-8 *speak . . . break* A common rhyme ('ea' = 'a' sound in 'bake'); cf. Thomas
     Morley's lyric, 'Now is the month of Maying'.
243-4 *build . . . child* Shakespeare rhymes 'child . . . spilled', *Romeo and Juliet*
     III.i.146-7.
244 *dry* barren

  5 *I* ed. (Q omits)
  6 *gameful* joyful

Get but his wife with child, perch at tree top,   10
And shake the golden fruit into her lap.
About it before she weep herself to a dry ground,
And whine out all her goodness.

TOUCHWOOD SENIOR
Prithee cease, I find a too much aptness in my blood
For such a business without provocation;   15
You might'well spared this banquet of eringoes,
Artichokes, potatoes, and your buttered crab;
They were fitter kept for your own wedding dinner.

TOUCHWOOD JUNIOR
Nay and you'll follow my suit, and save my purse too,
Fortune dotes on me; he's in happy case   20
Finds such an honest friend i'the common place.

TOUCHWOOD SENIOR
Life what makes thee so merry? Thou hast no cause
That I could hear of lately since thy crosses,
Unless there be news come, with new additions.

TOUCHWOOD JUNIOR
Why there thou hast it right: 25
I look for her this evening brother.

TOUCHWOOD SENIOR
How's that, look for her?

TOUCHWOOD JUNIOR
I will deliver you of the wonder straight brother:
By the firm secrecy and kind assistance
Of a good wench i'the house, who, made of pity,   30
Weighing the case her own, she's led through gutters,
Strange hidden ways, which none but love could find,
Or ha' the heart to venture; I expect her
Where you would little think.

10–11 *perch . . . lap* Plucking the golden apples borne by a tree in the Garden of the
    Hesperides, the daughters of Hesperus, was a common sexual metaphor; here the
    image is of a harvester shaking the fruit down while up the tree. Cf. *The
    Changeling* III.iii.174–5.
12 *weep . . . ground* before she loses her fertility
16 *might'well spared* might as well have spared
16–17 *eringoes . . . crab* All thought to be aphrodisiacs; 'eringo' was the candied
    fruit of sea holly, 'potato' was probably the sweet potato or yam. Cf. John
    Marston, *The Scourge of Villainy*, Satire III, ll. 67–74.
21 *friend i'the common place* a friend at the right time, 'a friend at court'; literally,
    the court of common pleas at Westminster
31 *gutters* roof gutters between houses. See IV.i.286.

TOUCHWOOD SENIOR   I care not where,
So she be safe, and yours.
TOUCHWOOD JUNIOR   Hope tells me so,   35
But from your love and time my peace must grow.   *Exit*
TOUCHWOOD SENIOR
You know the worst then brother. Now to my Kix,
The barren he and she; they're i'the next room,
But to say which of their two humours hold them
Now at this instant, I cannot say truly.   40
SIR OLIVER
Thou liest barrenness.   KIX *to his* LADY *within*
TOUCHWOOD SENIOR
O is't that time of day? Give you joy of your tongue,
There's nothing else good in you; this their life
The whole day from eyes open to eyes shut,
Kissing or scolding, and then must be made friends,   45
Then rail the second part of the first fit out,
And then be pleased again, no man knows which way,
Fall out like giants, and fall in like children –
Their fruit can witness as much.

Enter SIR OLIVER KIX *and his* LADY

SIR OLIVER
'Tis thy fault.   50
LADY KIX
Mine, drouth and coldness?
SIR OLIVER
Thine, 'tis thou art barren.
LADY KIX
I barren! O life that I durst but speak now
In mine own justice, in mine own right – I barren!
'Twas otherways with me when I was at court;   55
I was ne'er called so till I was married.
SIR OLIVER
I'll be divorced.

---

37 *worst* i.e. 'Things can only get better from now on.'
39 *humours* moods, dispositions
46 *fit* (a) struggle (b) section of song or poem
48 *fall in* (a) make up after a quarrel (b) have sex
51 *drouth* drought
55 *court* Another reference to loose living in high places; cf. V. C. Gildersleeve, *Government Regulation of Elizabethan Drama* (1908), p. 109.
57 *divorced* Sir Oliver would have found it difficult, as legislation was necessary for divorce; ecclesiastical courts could grant a separation for adultery or cruelty or annulment for an illegally contracted marriage but remarriage was forbidden.

LADY KIX　　　　　　Be hanged! I need not wish it,
That will come too soon to thee: I may say,
'Marriage and hanging goes by destiny',
For all the goodness I can find in't yet.　　　　　　　　60

SIR OLIVER
I'll give up house, and keep some fruitful whore,
Like an old bachelor in a tradesman's chamber;
She and her children shall have all.

LADY KIX
Where be they?

TOUCHWOOD SENIOR
[*Coming forward*] Pray cease;　　　　　　　　　　　65
When there are friendlier courses took for you
To get and multiply within your house,
At your own proper costs in spite of censure,
Methinks an honest peace might be established.

SIR OLIVER
What, with her? Never!　　　　　　　　　　　　70

TOUCHWOOD SENIOR
Sweet sir.

SIR OLIVER
You work all in vain.

LADY KIX
Then he doth all like thee.

TOUCHWOOD SENIOR
Let me intreat sir.

SIR OLIVER
Singleness confound her,　　　　　　　　　　　75
I took her with one smock.

LADY KIX
But indeed you came not so single,
When you came from shipboard.

SIR OLIVER
Heart she bit sore there;
Prithee make's friends.　　　　　　　　　　　　80

TOUCHWOOD SENIOR
Is't come to that? The peal begins to cease.

SIR OLIVER
I'll sell all at an outcry.

---

59 *Marriage . . . destiny* proverbial
68 *At . . . censure* 'At your own cost despite any social criticism'
76 *one smock* i.e. very little property
77 *single* celibate; possibly 'lousy'
82 *outcry* auction, proclaimed by the common crier

LADY KIX
    Do thy worst, slave!
    Good sweet sir, bring us into love again.

TOUCHWOOD SENIOR
    Some would think this impossible to compass;   85
    Pray let this storm fly over.

SIR OLIVER
    Good sir pardon me, I'm master of this house,
    Which I'll sell presently; I'll clap up bills this evening.

TOUCHWOOD SENIOR
    Lady, friends – come?

LADY KIX
    If e'er ye loved woman, talk not on't sir;   90
    What, friends with him? Good faith do you think I'm mad?
    With one that's scarce the hinder quarter of a man?

SIR OLIVER
    Thou art nothing of a woman.

LADY KIX
    Would I were less than nothing.   *Weeps*

SIR OLIVER
    Nay prithee what dost mean?   95

LADY KIX
    I cannot please you.

SIR OLIVER
    I'faith thou art a good soul, he lies that says it;
    Buss, buss, pretty rogue.

LADY KIX
    You care not for me.

TOUCHWOOD SENIOR
    Can any man tell now which way they came in?   100
    By this light I'll be hanged then.

SIR OLIVER
    Is the drink come?

TOUCHWOOD SENIOR
    Here's a little vial of almond-milk   *Aside*
    That stood me in some three pence.

SIR OLIVER
    I hope to see thee, wench, within these few years,   105
    Circled with children, pranking up a girl,

---

 88 *presently* at once
     clap up bills put up posters
103 *almond-milk* made from sweet almonds, pounded, with water, stirred into thick
       barley water, sweetened and boiled; used in milk puddings
104 *stood me in* cost me
106 *pranking up* dressing smartly

And putting jewels in their little ears;
Fine sport i'faith.

LADY KIX
Ay had you been aught, husband,
It had been done ere this time.   110

SIR OLIVER
Had I been aught? Hang thee, hadst thou been aught;
But a cross thing I ever found thee.

LADY KIX
Thou art a grub to say so.

SIR OLIVER
A pox on thee.

TOUCHWOOD SENIOR
By this light they are out again at the same door,   115
And no man can tell which way;
Come, here's your drink sir.

SIR OLIVER
I will not take it now sir,
And I were sure to get three boys ere midnight.

LADY KIX
Why there thou show'st now of what breed thou com'st;   120
To hinder generation! O thou villain,
That knows how crookedly the world goes with us
For want of heirs, yet put by all good fortune.

SIR OLIVER
Hang, strumpet, I will take it now in spite.

TOUCHWOOD SENIOR
Then you must ride upon't five hours.   125

SIR OLIVER
I mean so. Within there?

Enter a SERVANT

SERVANT
Sir?

SIR OLIVER
Saddle the white mare,

[*Exit* SERVANT]

I'll take a whore along, and ride to Ware.

---

107 *their* Dyce and Bullen emend to 'her', but both sexes wore earrings until about
1660.

109 *aught* anything

129 *Ware* twenty miles north of London, like Brentford a trysting place for lovers
legal and illicit; the Saracen's Head inn contained the Great Bed of Ware, 10 ft
9 in (3.3 m) square, now in the Victoria and Albert Museum, London

LADY KIX
    Ride to the devil.   130
SIR OLIVER
    I'll plague you every way;
    Look ye, do you see, 'tis gone.   *Drinks*
LADY KIX
    A pox go with it.
SIR OLIVER
    Ay, curse and spare not now.
TOUCHWOOD SENIOR
    Stir up and down sir, you must not stand.   135
SIR OLIVER
    Nay I'm not given to standing.
TOUCHWOOD SENIOR
    So much the better sir for the ——
SIR OLIVER
    I never could stand long in one place yet,
    I learnt it of my father, ever figient;
    How if I crossed this sir?   *Capers* 140
TOUCHWOOD SENIOR
    O passing good sir, and would show well a-horseback;
    when you come to your inn, if you leapt over a joint-stool
    or two 'twere not amiss – although you brake your neck sir.
                                         Aside
SIR OLIVER
    What say you to a table thus high sir?
TOUCHWOOD SENIOR
    Nothing better sir, if it be furnished with good victuals.   145
    You remember how the bargain runs about this business?
SIR OLIVER
    Or else I had a bad head: you must receive sir four hundred
    pounds of me at four several payments: one hundred pound
    now in hand.
TOUCHWOOD SENIOR
    Right, that I have sir.   150

---

136 *standing* (a) being still (b) keeping an erection
137 The lacuna here and others elsewhere in the play may indicate that the actor is
    to *ad lib*, or whisper to his listener; alternatively, that the Master of the Revels
    may have deleted a perceived obscenity.
139 *figient* restless, fidgety
140 *crossed* jumped across a table or chair
142 *joint-stool* solidly constructed of pieces fitted together, often carved, about 2 ft
    (60 cm) high; very common. Stool-leaping was a fashionable game.
147 *bad head* ironic reference to cuckold's horns

SIR OLIVER
  Another hundred when my wife is quick: the third when
  she's brought to bed: and the last hundred when the child
  cries; for if it should be stillborn, it doth no good sir.
TOUCHWOOD SENIOR
  All this is even still; a little faster sir.
SIR OLIVER
  Not a whit sir,   155
  I'm in an excellent pace for any physic.

                    Enter a SERVANT

SERVANT
  Your white mare's ready.
SIR OLIVER
  I shall up presently: one kiss, and farewell.
LADY KIX
  Thou shalt have two love.
SIR OLIVER
  Expect me about three.   160

                          Exit [with SERVANT]

LADY KIX
  With all my heart sweet.
TOUCHWOOD SENIOR
  By this light they have forgot their anger since,
  And are as far in again as e'er they were;
  Which way the devil came they? Heart I saw 'em not,
  Their ways are beyond finding out. Come sweet lady.   165
LADY KIX
  How must I take mine sir?
TOUCHWOOD SENIOR
  Clean contrary; yours must be taken lying.
LADY KIX
  Abed sir?
TOUCHWOOD SENIOR
  Abed, or where you will for your own ease;
  Your coach will serve.   170

151 *wife* ed. (wifes Q)
    quick pregnant
154 *even* exact
    faster Sir Oliver has been capering all this while.
156 *physic* medicine
162 *since* now
170 *coach* First introduced in 1564, coaches were popular by the early 17th century
    and Dekker remarks, 'close caroaches were made running bawdy-houses' (*The
    Owl's Almanac* (1618), p. 8).

LADY KIX   The physic must needs please.

                                                    Ex[eunt]

Act IV, [Scene i]

Enter TIM *and* TUTOR

TIM
  Negatur argumentum, tutor.
TUTOR
  Probo tibi, pupil, *stultus non est animal rationale.*
TIM
  Falleris sane.
TUTOR
  Quæso ut taceas, probo tibi –
TIM
  Quomodo probas domine?   5
TUTOR
  Stultus non habet rationem, ergo non est animal rationale.
TIM
  Sic argumentaris domine, stultus non habet rationem, ergo
  non est animal rationale, negatur argumentum again tutor.
TUTOR
  Argumentum iterum probo tibi domine, qui non participat
  de ratione nullo modo potest vocari rationalibus, but *stul-*   10

1–19 *Tim.* Your argument is denied, tutor. *Tut.* I am proving to you, pupil, that a
fool is not a rational animal. *Tim.* Indeed you will be wrong. *Tut.* I ask you to
be silent, I am showing you. *Tim.* How will you prove it, master? *Tut.* A fool has
no reason, therefore he is not a rational animal. *Tim.* Thus you argue, master, a
fool does not have reason, therefore he is not a reasonable animal; your argument is denied again, tutor. *Tut.* I will demonstrate the argument to you again,
sir: he who doesn't partake of reason can in no way be called rational, but a fool
does not partake of reason, therefore a fool can in no way be called rational.
Tim. He does partake. *Tut.* So you hold; how does the partaker partake? *Tim.*
As a man; I will prove it to you in a syllogism. *Tut.* Prove it. *Tim.* I prove it thus,
master: a fool is a man just as you and I are, man is a rational animal, just so a
fool is a rational animal.

tus non participat de ratione, ergo stultus nullo modo
potest dicere.

TIM
Participat.

TUTOR
Sic disputus, qui participat quomodo participat?

TIM
Ut homo, probabo tibi in syllogismo.   15

TUTOR
Hunc proba.

TIM
Sic probo domine, stultus est homo sicut tu et ego sum,
homo est animal rationale, sicut stultus est animal ration-
ale.

Enter MAUDLINE

MAUDLINE
Here's nothing but disputing all the day long with 'em.   20

TUTOR
Sic disputus, stultus est homo sicut tu et ego sum homo est
animal rationale, sicut stultus est animal rationale.

MAUDLINE
Your reasons are both good what e'er they be;
Pray give them o'er, faith you'll tire yourselves,
What's the matter between you?   25

TIM
Nothing but reasoning about a fool, mother.

MAUDLINE
About a fool, son? Alas what need you trouble your heads
about that, none of us all but knows what a fool is.

TIM
Why what's a fool, mother?
I come to you now.   30

MAUDLINE
Why one that's married before he has wit.

TIM
'Tis pretty i'faith, and well guessed of a woman never
brought up at the university: but bring forth what fool you

---

11 *de* (*ac* Folger Q)

21–2 *Tut.* So you contend: a fool is a man just as you and I are, man is a rational
       animal, just as a fool is a rational animal.

30 *I come to you* a term in academic disputation for 'I put the question to you'

31 *wit* (a) intelligence (b) penis

33 *bring forth* ironic, as Maudline brought forth Tim at his birth

will mother, I'll prove him to be as reasonable a creature as
myself or my tutor here.   35

MAUDLINE
Fie 'tis impossible.

TUTOR
Nay he shall do't forsooth.

TIM
'Tis the easiest thing to prove a fool by logic,
By logic I'll prove anything.

MAUDLINE
What thou wilt not?   40

TIM
I'll prove a whore to be an honest woman.

MAUDLINE
Nay by my faith, she must prove that herself, or logic will
never do't.

TIM
'Twill do't I tell you.

MAUDLINE
Some in this street would give a thousand pounds that you   45
could prove their wives so.

TIM
Faith I can, and all their daughters too, though they had
three bastards. When comes your tailor hither?

MAUDLINE
Why, what of him?

TIM
By logic I'll prove him to be a man,   50
Let him come when he will.

MAUDLINE
How hard at first was learning to him? Truly sir I thought
he would never a took the Latin tongue. How many
Accidences do you think he wore out ere he came to his
Grammar?   55

TUTOR
Some three or four?

MAUDLINE
Believe me sir, some four and thirty.

TIM
Pish, I made haberdines of 'em in church porches.

---

48 *tailor* Tailors, especially women's, were considered unmanly; cf. nursery rhyme,
    'Four and twenty tailors / Went to kill a snail', and note to II.ii.14.

54 *Accidences* books of the rudiments of Latin grammar; Tim was, not surprisingly,
    a slow learner it seems

58 *haberdines* salt dried codfish. Dyce suggests, 'Perhaps Tim alludes to some

MAUDLINE
He was eight years in his Grammar, and stuck horribly at a
foolish place there called *as in presenti*.   60

TIM
Pox I have it here now.

MAUDLINE
He so shamed me once before an honest gentleman that
knew me when I was a maid.

TIM
These women must have all out.

MAUDLINE
'*Quid est grammatica?*' Says the gentleman to him (I shall   65
remember by a sweet, sweet token), but nothing could he
answer.

TUTOR
How now pupil, ha, *quid est grammatica?*

TIM
Grammatica? Ha, ha, ha!

MAUDLINE
Nay do not laugh son, but let me hear you say it now: there   70
was one word went so prettily off the gentleman's tongue,
I shall remember it the longest day of my life.

TUTOR
Come, *quid est grammatica?*

TIM
Are you not ashamed tutor? *Grammatica?* Why, *recte
scribendi atque loquendi ars*, sir-reverence of my mother.   75

MAUDLINE
That was it i'faith: why now son I see you are a deep
scholar; and master tutor a word I pray, let us withdraw a

---

childish sport'. Frost suggests a game where cut-out fish shapes are blown over
a line on the floor; Parker cites a Christmas game, 'Selling of fish', and 'the
foolscap decorated with paper emblems of red herring worn by Jack-of-Lent'. As
'cod' = scrotum, however, this is the first of a series of *doubles entendres* concluded when Maudlin invites the tutor to 'withdraw a little into my husband's
chamber'.

60 *as in presenti* Introductory phrase in the part of Lily and Colet's *A Short
Introduction to Grammar* (1549) dealing with inflections of verbs; several
writers make puns on it, e.g. Marston, *What You Will*, II.i. Here the pun is on
both 'arse' (see l. 75) and 'cunt' (see l. 78).

64 *must have all out* must tell all, but with a sexual suggestion

65 *Quid est grammatica?* 'What is grammar?'

74–5 'The art of speaking and writing correctly'; (see J. D. Reeves, 'Middleton and
Lily's Grammar', *N&Q*, 197 (1952), 75–6).

75 *sir-reverence* (i) with apologies to (ii) excrement (continuing the pun on *as*)

little into my husband's chamber; I'll send in the North
Wales gentlewoman to him, she looks for wooing: I'll put
together both, and lock the door.   80

TUTOR

I give great approbation to your conclusion.

                                    Exit [with MAUDLINE]

TIM

I mar'l what this gentlewoman should be
That I should have in marriage, she's a stranger to me:
I wonder what my parents mean i'faith,
To match me with a stranger so: 85
A maid that's neither kiff nor kin to me:
Life, do they think I have no more care of my body
Than to lie with one that I ne'er knew,
A mere stranger,
One that ne'er went to school with me neither,   90
Nor ever playfellows together?
They're mightily o'erseen in't methinks;
They say she has mountains to her marriage,
She's full of cattle, some two thousand runts;
Now what the meaning of these runts should be,   95
My tutor cannot tell me;
I have looked in Rider's Dictionary for the letter R,
And there I can hear no tidings of these runts neither;
Unless they should be Rumford hogs,
I know them not,   100

                        Enter WELSH GENTLEWOMAN

And here she comes.
If I know what to say to her now
In the way of marriage, I'm no graduate;
Methinks i'faith 'tis boldly done of her
To come into my chamber being but a stranger;   105
She shall not say I'm so proud yet, but I'll speak to her:
Marry as I will order it,

---

80 *lock the door* Cf. Allwit's 'pin the door' I.ii.30.

83 *stranger* foreigner

86 *kiff* kith, neighbour (as in 'kith and kin')

92 *o'erseen* mistaken

94 *runts* small breed of Welsh and Highland cattle

97 *Rider's Dictionary* English-Latin and Latin-English dictionary compiled by the
    Bishop of Killaloe, John Rider, first published at Oxford in 1589.

99 *Rumford* (Romford) in Essex 12 miles (20 km) north-east of London, held hog
    markets on Tuesdays and grain and cattle markets on Wednesdays

She shall take no hold of my words I'll warrant her;
She looks and makes a curtsey –
Salve tu quoque puella pulcherrima,   110
Quid vis nescio nec sane curo –
Tully's own phrase to a heart.

WELSH GENTLEWOMAN

I know not what he means;
A suitor quotha?
I hold my life he understands no English.   115

TIM

Fertur me hercule tu virgo,
Wallia ut opibus abundis maximis.

WELSH GENTLEWOMAN

What's this *fertur* and *abundundis*?
He mocks me sure, and calls me a bundle of farts.

TIM

I have no Latin word now for their runts; I'll make some   120
shift or other: *Iterum dico opibus abundat maximis mon-*
tibus et fontibus et ut ita dicam rontibus, attamen vero
homanculus ego sum natura simule arte bachalarius lecto
profecto non parata.

WELSH GENTLEWOMAN

This is most strange; may be he can speak Welsh –   125
Avedera whee comrage, derdue cog foginis?

TIM

Cog foggin? I scorn to cog with her, I'll tell her so too, in a
word near her own language: *Ego non cogo.*

110–11 'Hail to you too, most beautiful maiden; what you want I don't know and
certainly don't care.'

112 *Tully's* Cicero's

114 *quotha?* said he? indeed?

116–17 'It's said, by Hercules, young lady, that Wales has the greatest abundance of
riches.'
  Fertur prounced 'Fartur'

121–4 'Again I say that you abound in resources, in the greatest mountains and foun-
tains and, as I could say, runts; however I am truly but a little chap by nature
and by art a bachelor, not actually ready for bed'. The Latin is by no means
clear. The reference to Tim's size indicates that the part was probably played by
one of the Queen's Revels boys.

126 'Can you speak Welsh, for God's sake are you pretending with me?' A phonetic
rendering for '*A fedrwch chwi Cymraeg, er Duw cog fo gennyf?*' (The final 's'
may be due to a misreading of the copytext.)

127 *Cog* Probably a pun on 'cog' = lie (deceive).

128 'I won't come together [with you].'

WELSH GENTLEWOMAN
  Rhegosin a whiggin harle ron corid ambre.
TIM
  By my faith she's a good scholar, I see that already;   130
  She has the tongues plain, I hold my life she has travelled;
  What will folks say? 'There goes the learned couple'!
  Faith if the truth were known, she hath proceeded.

Enter MAUDLINE

MAUDLINE
  How now, how speeds your business?
TIM
  I'm glad my mother's come to part us.   135
MAUDLINE
  How do you agree forsooth?
WELSH GENTLEWOMAN
  As well as e'er we did before we met.
MAUDLINE
  How's that?
WELSH GENTLEWOMAN
  You put me to a man I understand not;
  Your son's no English man methinks.   140
MAUDLINE
  No English man! Bless my boy,
  And born i'the heart of London?
WELSH GENTLEWOMAN
  I ha' been long enough in the chamber with him,
  And I find neither Welsh nor English in him.
MAUDLINE
  Why Tim, how have you used the gentlewoman?   145
TIM
  As well as a man might do, mother, in modest Latin.
MAUDLINE
  Latin, fool?
TIM
  And she recoiled in Hebrew.
MAUDLINE
  In Hebrew, fool? 'Tis Welsh.
TIM
  All comes to one, mother.   150

---

129 The first part could mean 'Some cheese and whey after a walk', a phonetic ren-
    dering of '*Rhyn gosyn a chwig gin ar ôl bod yn cerdedd am dro*'. The Welsh were
    popularly thought to delight in cheese.
133 *proceeded* (a) graduated (b) gone past virginity
148 *recoiled* answered

MAUDLINE
  She can speak English too.

TIM
  Who told me so much?
  Heart, and she can speak English, I'll clap to her,
  I thought you'd marry me to a stranger.

MAUDLINE
  You must forgive him, he's so inured to Latin,   155
  He and his tutor, that he hath quite forgot
  To use the Protestant tongue.

WELSH GENTLEWOMAN
  'Tis quickly pardoned forsooth.

MAUDLINE
  Tim make amends and kiss her,
  He makes towards you forsooth.   160

TIM
  O delicious, one may discover her country by her kissing.
  'Tis a true saying, there's nothing tastes so sweet as your
  Welsh mutton. It was reported you could sing.

MAUDLINE
  O rarely Tim, the sweetest British songs.

TIM
  And 'tis my mind, I swear, before I marry   165
  I would see all my wife's good parts at once,
  To view how rich I were.

MAUDLINE
  Thou shalt hear sweet music Tim.
  Pray, forsooth.   *Music and Welsh song*
[WELSH GENTLEWOMAN *sings*]

The Song

    Cupid is Venus' only joy,   170
    But he is a wanton boy,
    A very, very wanton boy,
    He shoots at ladies' naked breasts,
    He is the cause of most men's crests,

153 *clap* clasp, stick closely to, with a hidden irony as 'clap' also = pox
157 *Protestant tongue* English
161 *country* a familiar pun (cf. *Hamlet*, III.ii.121)
163 *Welsh mutton* was famous, but Tim's speech is all unconscious *double entendre*:
    cf. I.i.140
    sing used again with a sexual sense; cf. II.i.52
170–95 The first nine lines of this song, with two additional lines, occur in
    Middleton's *More Dissemblers Besides Women*, I.iv.
174 *crests* cuckolds' horns

    I mean upon the forehead,   175
    Invisible but horrid;
    'Twas he first taught upon the way
    To keep a lady's lips in play.

    Why should not Venus chide her son,
    For the pranks that he hath done,   180
    The wanton pranks that he hath done?
    He shoots his fiery darts so thick,
    They hurt poor ladies to the quick,
    Ah me, with cruel wounding;
    His darts are so confounding,   185
    That life and sense would soon decay,
    But that he keeps their lips in play.

    Can there be any part of bliss,
    In a quickly fleeting kiss,
    A quickly fleeting kiss?   190
    To one's pleasure, leisures are but waste,
    The slowest kiss makes too much haste,
    And lose it ere we find it,
    The pleasing sport they only know,
    That close above and close below.   195

TIM
    I would not change my wife for a kingdom;
    I can do somewhat too in my own lodging.

       Enter YELLOWHAMMER *and* ALLWIT

YELLOWHAMMER
    Why well said Tim, the bells go merrily,
    I love such peals a-life; wife lead them in a while,
    Here's a strange gentleman desires private conference.   200

    [*Exeunt* MAUDLINE, TIM *and* WELSH GENTLEWOMAN]

    You're welcome sir, the more for your name's sake.
    Good Master Yellowhammer, I love my name well;
    And which o'the Yellowhammers take you descent from,
    If I may be so bold with you, which, I pray?

183 *quick* tenderest part, but with a bawdy implication
187 *lips* those above and below
194 Frost adds a line here to equalize the stanzas.
197 *lodging* 'on my own account', but with a bawdy pun; Bullen unnecessarily adds
    s.d. *Sings.*
199 *a-life* as my life; extremely

ALLWIT
The Yellowhammers in Oxfordshire,   205
Near Abbington.

YELLOWHAMMER
And those are the best Yellowhammers, and truest bred: I
came from thence myself, though now a citizen: I'll be bold
with you: you are most welcome.

ALLWIT
I hope the zeal I bring with me shall deserve it.   210

YELLOWHAMMER
I hope no less; what is your will sir?

ALLWIT
I understand by rumours, you have a daughter,
Which my bold love shall henceforth title 'cousin'.

YELLOWHAMMER
I thank you for her sir.

ALLWIT
I heard of her virtues, and other confirmed graces.   215

YELLOWHAMMER
A plaguy girl sir.

ALLWIT
Fame sets her out with richer ornaments
Than you are pleased to boast of; 'tis done modestly.
I hear she's towards marriage.

YELLOWHAMMER
You hear truth sir.   220

ALLWIT
And with a knight in town, Sir Walter Whorehound.

YELLOWHAMMER
The very same sir.

ALLWIT
I am the sorrier for't.

YELLOWHAMMER
The sorrier? Why cousin?

ALLWIT
'Tis not too far past is't? It may be yet recalled?   225

YELLOWHAMMER
Recalled, why good sir?

ALLWIT
Resolve me in that point, ye shall hear from me.

---

206 *Abbington* (Abingdon), in Berkshire, on the Thames 56 miles (90 km) north-west
   of London; six miles (10 km) south of Oxford
227 *Resolve . . . point* Satisfy me

YELLOWHAMMER
  There's no contract passed.

ALLWIT
  I am very joyful sir.

YELLOWHAMMER
  But he's the man must bed her.   230

ALLWIT
  By no means coz, she's quite undone then,
  And you'll curse the time that e'er you made the match;
  He's an arrant whoremaster, consumes his time and state,
  —— whom in my knowledge he hath kept this seven years,
  Nay coz, another man's wife too.   235

YELLOWHAMMER
  O abominable!

ALLWIT
  Maintains the whole house, apparels the husband,
  Pays servants' wages, not so much, but ——

YELLOWHAMMER
  Worse and worse, and doth the husband know this?

ALLWIT
  Knows? Ay and glad he may too: 'tis his living;   240
  As other trades thrive, butchers by selling flesh,
  Poulters by venting conies, or the like, coz.

YELLOWHAMMER
  What an incomparable wittol's this?

ALLWIT
  Tush, what cares he for that?
  Believe me coz, no more than I do.   245

YELLOWHAMMER
  What a base slave is that?

ALLWIT
  All's one to him; he feeds and takes his ease,
  Was ne'er the man that ever broke his sleep
  To get a child yet by his own confession,
  And yet his wife has seven.   250

YELLOWHAMMER
  What, by Sir Walter?

---

228 *contract* A *de praesenti* contract of marriage was made by two people agreeing
     before witnesses to take each other as man and wife and was held to be binding
     (cf. Webster, *The Duchess of Malfi*, II.i.392); a contract *de futuro* was an agree-
     ment to marry in the future and could be broken.
     passed (past Q)

234 The lacunae here and four lines further on are in Q; see note to III.iii.137.

242 *Poulters* (a) Sellers of birds (b) Bawds
     venting conies selling (a) rabbits (b) prostitutes

ALLWIT
　　Sir Walter's like to keep 'em, and maintain 'em,
　　In excellent fashion, he dares do no less sir.
YELLOWHAMMER
　　Life has he children too?
ALLWIT
　　Children? Boys thus high,   255
　　In their Cato and Cordelius.
YELLOWHAMMER
　　What, you jest sir!
ALLWIT
　　Why, one can make a verse,
　　And is now at Eton College.
YELLOWHAMMER
　　O this news has cut into my heart coz.   260
ALLWIT
　　It had eaten nearer if it had not been prevented.
　　One Allwit's wife.
YELLOWHAMMER
　　Allwit? Foot, I have heard of him;
　　He had a girl kursened lately?
ALLWIT
　　Ay, that work did cost the knight above a hundred mark.   265
YELLOWHAMMER
　　I'll mark him for a knave and villain for't!
　　A thousand thanks and blessings, I have done with him.
ALLWIT
　　[Aside] Ha, ha, ha, this knight will stick by my ribs still,
　　I shall not lose him yet, no wife will come;
　　Where'er he woos, I find him still at home, ha, ha!   Exit 270
YELLOWHAMMER
　　Well grant all this, say now his deeds are black,
　　Pray what serves marriage; but to call him back;
　　I have kept a whore myself, and had a bastard,
　　By Mistress Anne, in Anno —
　　I care not who knows it; he's now a jolly fellow,   275

---

256 *Cato and Cordelius* Dionysius Cato's *Disticha de Moribus,* written in the 3rd or
　　4th century, and Marthurin Cordier's *Colloquia scholastica* (1564) were famous
　　textbooks, approved by Puritans.
259 *Eton College* founded by Henry VI in 1440, in Buckinghamshire some 23 miles
　　(38 km) west of London on the Thames opposite Windsor
261 *prevented* anticipated
263 *Foot* God's foot
272 *call him back* reform him
274 *in Anno* 'in the year', punning on the mother's name

H'as been twice warden, so may his fruit be,
They were but base begot, and so was he;
The knight is rich, he shall be my son-in-law
No matter so the whore he keeps be wholesome,
My daughter takes no hurt then; so let them wed,   280
I'll have him sweat well e'er they go to bed.

Enter MAUDLINE

MAUDLINE
O husband! Husband!
YELLOWHAMMER
How now Maudline?
MAUDLINE
We are all undone, she's gone, she's gone.
YELLOWHAMMER
Again? Death which way?   285
MAUDLINE
Over the houses:
Lay the waterside, she's gone forever else.
YELLOWHAMMER
O venturous baggage!

Exit [*with* MAUDLINE]

Enter TIM *and* TUTOR

TIM
Thieves, thieves, my sister's stol'n!
Some thief hath got her: 290
O how miraculously did my father's plate 'scape!
'Twas all left out, tutor.
TUTOR
Is't possible?
TIM
Besides three chains of pearl and a box of coral.
My sister's gone, let's look at Trig stairs for her;   295

276 *warden* (a) see note II.i.71 (b) a pear, taken up punningly in *fruit*. Pears were sex-
     ually symbolic; cf. *Romeo and Juliet* II.i.37.
     his Sir Walter's
277 *They* Sir Walter's children by Mrs Allwit
279 *wholesome* free of the pox
281 *sweat well* in a steam tub to cure any venereal disease
287 *Lay* Set watch on
295 *Trig stairs* a landing place on the Thames at the bottom of Trig Lane; appropri-
     ate for Tim, as *trig* was slang for a coxcomb, a dandified fool

My mother's gone to lay the Common stairs
At Puddle wharf, and at the dock below
Stands my poor silly father. Run sweet tutor, run.

Exit [with TUTOR]

[Act IV, Scene ii]

Enter both the TOUCHWOODS

TOUCHWOOD SENIOR
I had been taken brother by eight sergeants,
But for the honest watermen; I am bound to them,
They are the most requiteful'st people living,
For as they get their means by gentlemen,
They are still the forwardest to help gentlemen.   5
You heard how one 'scaped out of the Blackfriars,
But a while since from two or three varlets
Came into the house with all their rapiers drawn,
As if they'd dance the sword dance on the stage,
With candles in their hands like chandlers' ghosts,   10
Whilst the poor gentleman so pursued and bandied
Was by an honest pair of oars safely landed.
TOUCHWOOD JUNIOR
I love them with my heart for't.

296–7 *Common stairs at Puddle wharf* about two hundred yards upstream from Trig
    stairs; appropriate for Maudline. The 'dock' is presumably Dung wharf, down-
    stream, where the garbage was dumped onto barges. The reference continues the
    cloacan stream of scatological references in the play.
298 *silly* pitiable, helpless

  1 *sergeants* sheriff's officers
  2 *watermen* the taxicab men of the time. John Taylor, the 'water-poet', reckoned
    that by 1614 2,000 small boats plied the river about London and between
    Windsor and Gravesend; 40,000 lives were maintained by their labour.
    Queenhithe was their headquarters and they were renowned for strong language.
  3 *most requiteful'st* most willing to return favours
  6 *Blackfriars* theatre, the second known 'private' theatre, indoors and lit by can-
    dles; used by boys' companies 1600–08 and by the King's Men 1608–42.
  9 *sword dance* Among the different kinds of sword dances included in plays of the
    time were adaptations of folk dances and choreographed mock fights.
 10 *candles* Ghosts carried symbolic objects so that they could be recognized; the ruf-
    fians needed candles to find their victim in the indoors Blackfriars theatre.
 11 *bandied* hit at, struck to and fro

Enter three or four WATERMEN

1 WATERMAN
Your first man sir.

2 WATERMAN
Shall I carry you gentlemen with a pair of oars?   15

TOUCHWOOD SENIOR
These be the honest fellows;
Take one pair, and leave the rest for her.

TOUCHWOOD JUNIOR
Barn Elms.

TOUCHWOOD SENIOR
No more brother.   [*Exit*]

1 WATERMAN
Your first man.   20

2 WATERMAN
Shall I carry your worship?

TOUCHWOOD JUNIOR
Go, and you honest watermen that stay,
Here's a French crown for you;
There comes a maid with all speed to take water,
Row her lustily to Barn Elms after me.   25

2 WATERMAN
To Barn Elms, good sir: make ready the boat Sam,
We'll wait below.

                              Ex[*eunt* WATERMEN]

Enter MOLL

TOUCHWOOD JUNIOR
What made you stay so long?

MOLL
I found the way more dangerous than I looked for.

TOUCHWOOD JUNIOR
Away quick, there's a boat waits for you,   30
And I'll take water at Paul's wharf, and overtake you.

MOLL
Good sir do, we cannot be too safe.

                                        [*Exeunt*]

14 *Your first man* the watermen's trade cry
18 *Barn Elms* a park and manor house upstream opposite Hammersmith, well-
   known for assignations and duels
23 *French crown* French *écu*, worth about the same as the English crown (5
   shillings)
24 *take water* A bawdy pun; cf. Touchwood Senior's 'water' at II.i.188.
31 *Paul's wharf* was between Puddle wharf and Trig stairs

Enter SIR WALTER, YELLOWHAMMER, TIM *and* TUTOR

SIR WALTER
Life, call you this close keeping?
YELLOWHAMMER
She was kept under a double lock.
SIR WALTER
A double devil.   35
TIM
That's a buff sergeant, tutor, he'll ne'er wear out.
YELLOWHAMMER
How would you have women locked?
TIM
With padlocks father, the Venetian uses it,
My tutor reads it.
SIR WALTER
Heart, if she were so locked up, how got she out?   40
YELLOWHAMMER
There was a little hole looked into the gutter,
But who would have dreamt of that?
SIR WALTER
A wiser man would.
TIM
He says true, father, a wise man for love will seek every
hole: my tutor knows it.   45
TUTOR
Verum poeta dicit.
TIM
Dicit Virgilius, father.
YELLOWHAMMER
Prithee talk of thy gills somewhere else, she's played the gill
with me: where's your wise mother now?

---

36 *buff* tough, whitish oxhide leather usually worn by sergeants
38 *Venetian* women were believed lascivious and weak and the men cruel and
    oppressive, using *padlocks* on doors and chastity belts.
39 *reads* advises, or in the normal sense; cf. 'The sly Venetian locked his lady's ware,
    / Yet through her wit Actaeon's badge he bare' (*Ariosto's Satires*, [Tr.] G.
    Markham (1608), sig. K2r); Actaeon was transformed into a horned stag for
    watching the goddess Artemis bathing.
41 *looked* opened
45 *knows* Ironic; as the tutor has cuckolded Yellowhammer.
46–7 'The poet speaks truth'; 'Virgil says it'. Tim is confusing the very moral Virgil
    with the more erotic Ovid.
48 *gill* wench

TIM

Run mad I think, I thought she would have drowned her-　　50
self; she would not stay for oars, but took a smelt boat: sure
I think she be gone a-fishing for her.

YELLOWHAMMER

She'll catch a goodly dish of gudgeons now,
Will serve us all to supper.

Enter MAUDLINE *drawing* MOLL *by the hair, and*
WATERMEN

MAUDLINE

I'll tug thee home by the hair.　　　　　　　　　　　　55

WATERMEN

Good mistress, spare her.

MAUDLINE

Tend your own business.

WATERMEN

You are a cruel mother.

Ex[eunt WATERMEN]

MOLL

O my heart dies!

MAUDLINE

I'll make thee an example for all the neighbours' daughters.　60

MOLL

Farewell life.

MAUDLINE

You that have tricks can counterfeit.

YELLOWHAMMER

Hold, hold Maudline!

MAUDLINE

I have brought your jewel by the hair.

YELLOWHAMMER

She's here knight.　　　　　　　　　　　　　　　　65

SIR WALTER

Forbear or I'll grow worse.

TIM

Look on her, tutor, she hath brought her from the water
like a mermaid; she's but half my sister now, as far as the
flesh goes, the rest may be sold to fishwives.

---

51 *smelt* any small and easily caught fish, therefore applied, like *gudgeon*, to a simpleton
53–4 'She'll make us all look fools'
68–9 *mermaid . . . fishwives* More unconscious irony; *mermaid* could mean 'whore',
and *fishwife*, 'bawd'.

MAUDLINE
Dissembling cunning baggage!   70
YELLOWHAMMER
Impudent strumpet!
SIR WALTER
Either give over both, or I'll give over:
Why have you used me thus unkind mistress?
Wherein have I deserved?
YELLOWHAMMER
You talk too fondly sir. We'll take another course and pre-   75
vent all; we might have done't long since; we'll lose no time
now, nor trust to't any longer: tomorrow morn as early as
sunrise we'll have you joined.
MOLL
O bring me death tonight, love pitying fates,
Let me not see tomorrow up upon the world.   80
YELLOWHAMMER
Are you content sir, till then she shall be watched?
MAUDLINE
Baggage you shall.

Exit [with MOLL *and* YELLOWHAMMER]

TIM
Why father, my tutor and I will both watch in armour.
TUTOR
How shall we do for weapons?
TIM
Take you no care for that, if need be I can send for con-   85
quering metal tutor, ne'er lost day yet; 'tis but at
Westminster – I am acquainted with him that keeps the
monuments; I can borrow Harry the Fifth's sword, 'twill
serve us both to watch with.

Exit [with TUTOR]

SIR WALTER
I never was so near my wish, as this chance   90
Makes me; ere tomorrow noon,
I shall receive two thousand pound in gold,
And a sweet maidenhead

---

87 *Westminster* The Abbey monuments could be viewed for a penny. Tim's foolishness is exposed again, since Henry V's armour had been stolen, with his head
of silver, though Edward III's sword was still there.

Worth forty.

Enter TOUCHWOOD JUNIOR *with a* WATERMAN

TOUCHWOOD JUNIOR
O thy news splits me.   95
WATERMAN
Half drowned, she cruelly tugged her by the hair,
Forced her disgracefully, not like a mother.
TOUCHWOOD JUNIOR
Enough, leave me like my joys.

Exit WATERMAN

Sir, saw you not a wretched maid pass this way?
Heart villain, is it thou?

Both draw and fight

SIR WALTER   Yes slave, 'tis I.   100
TOUCHWOOD JUNIOR
I must break through thee then, there is no stop
That checks my tongue and all my hopeful fortunes,
That breast excepted, and I must have way.
SIR WALTER
Sir, I believe 'twill hold your life in play.

[*Wounds* TOUCHWOOD JUNIOR]

TOUCHWOOD JUNIOR
Sir, you'll gain the heart in my breast at first?   105
SIR WALTER
There is no dealing then? Think on the dowry for two
thousand pounds.
TOUCHWOOD JUNIOR   [*Wounds* SIR WALTER]
O now 'tis quit sir.
SIR WALTER
Being of even hand, I'll play no longer.

94 *forty* Later in the 17th century 150 gold *écus* (about £37) and a year's keep were
   quoted as the price of a virgin in Venice. (See F. Henriques, *Prostitution and
   Society* (1963) II, p. 89).
102 *checks my tongue* stops me speaking; Touchwood Junior is also likening himself to a
   dog following a scent, 'giving tongue', and playing on his adversary's name; cf. I.i.143.
104 *in play* at risk. This begins a series of gaming images. Middleton later used such
   imagery with great effect in *Women Beware Women* II.ii, when the conversation
   during a chess game forms an ironic commentary on a seduction.
105 *Sir . . . first?* (first Q) 'You think you're going to stab me through the heart
   straight off?'
106–7 Sir Walter is offering Touchwood Junior a compromise deal allowing him to
   share in the dowry.

TOUCHWOOD JUNIOR
  No longer, slave?   110
SIR WALTER
  I have certain things to think on,
  Before I dare go further.
TOUCHWOOD JUNIOR
  But one bout?
  I'll follow thee to death, but ha't out.

Ex[eunt]

Act V, [Scene i]

Enter ALLWIT, *his* WIFE, *and* DAVY DAHUMMA

MISTRESS ALLWIT
  A misery of a house.
ALLWIT
  What shall become of us?
DAVY
  I think his wound be mortal.
ALLWIT
  Think'st thou so Davy?
  Then am I mortal too, but a dead man Davy;   5
  This is no world for me, when e'er he goes,
  I must e'en truss up all, and after him Davy,
  A sheet with two knots, and away.

Enter SIR WALTER *led in hurt*

DAVY   O see sir,
  How faint he goes, two of my fellows lead him.
MISTRESS ALLWIT
  O me!   [*Swoons*]   10
ALLWIT
  Hyday, my wife's laid down too, here's like to be
  A good house kept, when we are altogether down;
  Take pains with her good Davy, cheer her up there,
  Let me come to his worship, let me come.
SIR WALTER
  Touch me not villain, my wound aches at thee,   15
  Thou poison to my heart.

---

7 *truss up all* pack up everything
8 *sheet* a shroud, with knots at the head and feet

ALLWIT   He raves already,
  His senses are quite gone, he knows me not;
  Look up an't like your worship, heave those eyes,
  Call me to mind, is your remembrance left?
  Look in my face, who am I an't like your worship?   20
SIR WALTER
  If any thing be worse than slave or villain,
  Thou art the man.
ALLWIT   Alas his poor worship's weakness,
  He will begin to know me by little and little.
SIR WALTER
  No devil can be like thee.
ALLWIT   Ah poor gentleman,
  Methinks the pain that thou endurest –   25
SIR WALTER
  Thou know'st me to be wicked, for thy baseness
  Kept the eyes open still on all my sins,
  None knew the dear account my soul stood charged with
  So well as thou, yet like Hell's flattering angel
  Would'st never tell me on't, let'st me go on,   30
  And join with death in sleep, that if I had not waked
  Now by chance, even by a stranger's pity,
  I had everlastingly slept out all hope
  Of grace and mercy.
ALLWIT   Now he is worse and worse,
  Wife, to him wife, thou wast wont to do good on him.   35
MISTRESS ALLWIT
  How is't with you sir?
SIR WALTER   Not as with you,
  Thou loathsome strumpet! Some good pitying man
  Remove my sins out of my sight a little;
  I tremble to behold her, she keeps back
  All comfort while she stays; is this a time,   40
  Unconscionable woman, to see thee?
  Art thou so cruel to the peace of man,
  Not to give liberty now? The devil himself
  Shows a far fairer reverence and respect
  To goodness than thyself; he dares not do this,   45
  But parts in time of penitence, hides his face;

18, 20 *an't like* if it pleases
25 *Methinks* I think. Dyce added 'mads thee' to complete the line, Q has 'endurest',
    Parker emends 'endurest—', which makes good sense, with Sir Walter interrupt-
    ing Allwit.
35 *do good* with a pun on 'do' = copulate
46 *parts* (part Q) departs

When man withdraws from him, he leaves the place;
Hast thou less manners, and more impudence,
Than thy instructor? Prithee show thy modesty,
If the least grain be left, and get thee from me.   50
Thou should'st be rather locked many rooms hence,
From the poor miserable sight of me,
If either love or grace had part in thee.

MISTRESS ALLWIT
    He is lost for ever.
ALLWIT   Run sweet Davy quickly,
    And fetch the children hither – sight of them   55
    Will make him cheerful straight.

                                        [*Exit* DAVY]

SIR WALTER   O death! Is this
    A place for you to weep? What tears are those?
    Get you away with them, I shall fare the worse
    As long as they are a-weeping; they work against me;
    There's nothing but thy appetite in that sorrow,   60
    Thou weep'st for lust, I feel it in the slackness
    Of comforts coming towards me;
    I was well till thou began'st to undo me;
    This shows like the fruitless sorrow of a careless mother
    That brings her son with dalliance to the gallows,   65
    And then stands by, and weeps to see him suffer.

                    Enter DAVY *with the* CHILDREN

DAVY
    There are the children sir, an't like your worship;
    Your last fine girl, in troth she smiles,
    Look, look, in faith sir.
SIR WALTER   O my vengeance!
    Let me for ever hide my cursed face   70
    From sight of those, that darkens all my hopes,
    And stands between me and the sight of Heaven;
    Who sees me now, he too and those so near me,
    May rightly say, I am o'er-grown with sin;
    O how my offences wrestle with my repentance;   75
    It hath scarce breath –
    Still my adulterous guilt hovers aloft,

---

65 *dalliance* over-indulgence
69 *vengeance* God's vengeance, as represented in the children before him
73 *he* (ho Q); Dyce emends 'O too', Bullen 'O, O', George 'go to', Parker 'her too',
   but 'he' is acceptable, referring to (a) God, who 'sees [Sir Walter] now' or (b)
   'who[ever]'

And with her black wings beats down all my prayers
Ere they be half way up; what's he knows now
How long I have to live? O what comes then?   80
My taste grows bitter, the round world, all gall now,
Her pleasing pleasures now hath poisoned me,
Which I exchanged my soul for:
Make way a hundred sighs at once for me.

ALLWIT
Speak to him Nick.

NICK   I dare not, I am afraid.   85

ALLWIT
Tell him he hurts his wounds Wat, with making moan.

SIR WALTER
Wretched, death of seven.

ALLWIT
Come let's be talking somewhat to keep him alive.
Ah sirrah Wat, and did my lord bestow that jewel on thee,
For an epistle thou mad'st in Latin?   90
Thou art a good forward boy, there's great joy on thee.

SIR WALTER
O sorrow!

ALLWIT   Heart, will nothing comfort him?
If he be so far gone, 'tis time to moan;
Here's pen, and ink, and paper, and all things ready,
Will't please your worship for to make your will?   95

SIR WALTER
My will? Yes, yes, what else? Who writes apace now?

ALLWIT
That can your man Davy an't like your worship,
A fair, fast, legible hand.

SIR WALTER
Set it down then:
Imprimis, I bequeath to yonder wittol,   100
Three times his weight in curses.

ALLWIT
How?

SIR WALTER
All plagues of body and of mind –

ALLWIT
Write them not down Davy.

DAVY
It is his will, I must.   105

---

84 'Let a hundred sighs of repentance make a way (to heaven) for me'.
87 *seven* Mrs Allwit's children by Sir Walter
100 *Imprimis* In the first place

SIR WALTER
  Together also,
  With such a sickness, ten days ere his death.
ALLWIT
  [*Aside*] There's a sweet legacy,
  I am almost choked with't.
SIR WALTER
  Next I bequeath to that foul whore his wife,   110
  All barrenness of joy, a drouth of virtue,
  And dearth of all repentance: for her end,
  The common misery of an English strumpet,
  In French and Dutch, beholding ere she dies
  Confusion of her brats before her eyes,   115
  And never shed a tear for it.

                     Enter a SERVANT

SERVANT   Where's the knight?
  O sir, the gentleman you wounded is newly departed.
SIR WALTER
  Dead? Lift, lift, who helps me?
ALLWIT
  Let the law lift you now, that must have all,
  I have done lifting on you, and my wife too.   120
SERVANT
  You were best lock yourself close.
ALLWIT   Not in my house sir,
  I'll harbour no such persons as men-slayers,
  Lock yourself where you will –
SIR WALTER   What's this?
MISTRESS ALLWIT   Why husband!
ALLWIT
  I know what I do wife.
MISTRESS ALLWIT   You cannot tell yet;
  For having killed the man in his defence,   125
  Neither his life, nor estate will be touched, husband.
ALLWIT
  Away wife! Hear a fool! His lands will hang him.

114 *French* The 'French disease' was syphilis.
      Dutch probably sexually transmitted disease also, as a 'Dutch widow' was a
      harlot (see Middleton's *A Trick to Catch the Old One* III.iii.15–17), but it could
      refer to drunkenness
115 *Confusion* Shaming. Cf. Psalm 109:29 'Let mine adversaries be clothed with
      shame, and let them cover themselves with their own confusion . . .'
120 *lifting* (a) assisting (b) stealing (c) fucking
127 *Hear a fool* Listen to the silly woman! *lands* His lands will be forfeited to the
      Crown, since he's a murderer, so he is more likely to hang.

SIR WALTER
 Am I denied a chamber?
 What say you forsooth?

MISTRESS ALLWIT
 Alas sir, I am one that would have all well,   130
 But must obey my husband. Prithee love
 Let the poor gentleman stay, being so sore wounded;
 There's a close chamber at one end of the garret
 We never use, let him have that I prithee.

ALLWIT
 We never use? You forget sickness then,   135
 And physic times: is't not a place of easement?

Enter a SERVANT

SIR WALTER
 O death ! Do I hear this with part
 Of former life in me? What's the news now?

SERVANT
 Troth worse and worse, you're like to lose your land
 If the law save your life sir, or the surgeon.   140

ALLWIT
 Hark you there wife.

SIR WALTER
 Why how sir?

SERVANT
 Sir Oliver Kix's wife is new quickened;
 That child undoes you sir.

SIR WALTER   All ill at once.

ALLWIT
 I wonder what he makes here with his consorts?   145
 Cannot our house be private to ourselves,
 But we must have such guests? I pray depart sirs,
 And take your murderer along with you –
 Good he were apprehended ere he go,
 He's killed some honest gentleman. Send for officers!   150

SIR WALTER
 I'll soon save you that labour.

ALLWIT   I must tell you sir,
 You have been somewhat bolder in my house

---

133 *close chamber* secluded room, here the *place of easement*, the lavatory
145 *consorts* companions (i.e. his two servants)
150 *officers* of the watch could arrest offenders and take them before the constable
     or justice of the peace

Than I could well like of; I suffered you
Till it stuck here at my heart; I tell you truly
I thought you had been familiar with my wife once.   155

MISTRESS ALLWIT
With me? I'll see him hanged first; I defy him,
And all such gentlemen in the like extremity.

SIR WALTER
If ever eyes were open, these are they;
Gamesters farewell, I have nothing left to play.

Exit [with SERVANTS]

ALLWIT
And therefore get you gone sir.

DAVY   Of all wittols,   160
Be thou the head. Thou the grand whore of spitals.   *Exit*

ALLWIT
So since he's like now to be rid of all,
I am right glad I am so well rid of him.

MISTRESS ALLWIT
I knew he durst not stay, when you named officers.

ALLWIT
That stopped his spirits straight.   165
What shall we do now wife?

MISTRESS ALLWIT
As we were wont to do.

ALLWIT
We are richly furnished, wife, with household stuff.

MISTRESS ALLWIT
Let's let out lodgings then,
And take a house in the Strand.

ALLWIT   In troth a match wench: 170
We are simply stocked with cloth of tissue cushions,
To furnish out bay windows: push, what not that's quaint
And costly, from the top to the bottom.

---

159 *Gamesters* (a) Gamblers (b) Lechers
161 *spitals* places for the indigent and foully diseased (cf. note to II.i.146). 'To rob
      the spital' = to make gain or profit in a particularly mean or dastardly manner.
170 *Strand* the most fashionable part of London, running from Temple Bar to
      Charing Cross; a resort of high class whores
171 *simply* absolutely
172 *bay windows* were used by whores to display themselves (cf. Middleton, *Hengist,
      King of Kent* III.i.143); Allwit's use of 'quaint' (= cunt) indicates an intention
      of setting up a brothel.

Life, for furniture, we may lodge a countess:
There's a close-stool of tawny velvet too,   175
Now I think on't wife.

MISTRESS ALLWIT   There's that should be sir;
Your nose must be in every thing.

ALLWIT   I have done wench;
And let this stand in every gallant's chamber:
There's no gamester like a politic sinner,
For who e'er games, the box is sure a winner.   180

Exit [with MISTRESS ALLWIT]

[Act V, Scene ii]

Enter YELLOWHAMMER *and his* WIFE

MAUDLINE
O husband, husband, she will die, she will die,
There is no sign but death.

YELLOWHAMMER   'Twill be our shame then.

MAUDLINE
O how she's changed in compass of an hour.

YELLOWHAMMER
Ah my poor girl! Good faith thou wert too cruel
To drag her by the hair.   5

MAUDLINE
You would have done as much sir,
To curb her of her humour.

YELLOWHAMMER
'Tis curbed sweetly, she catched her bane o'th' water.

Enter TIM

MAUDLINE
How now Tim?

175 *close-stool* a chamber pot in a stool or box
176 *There's that . . . There's* everything there ought to be
180 *box* the box into which money was placed by gamesters as a kind of cover
    charge; 'every player, at the first hand he draweth, payeth a crown to the box,
    by the way of relief towards the house charges' (G. Walker, *A Manifest
    Detection of the Most Vile and Detestable Use of Diceplay*, ed. J. O. Halliwell
    (1850), p. 12) Allwit is comparing himself to the box, which no matter what
    happens, contains the money. There may also be a pun on box = coffin.

8 *water* pun on 'Walter'

TIM

    Faith busy, mother, about an epitaph   10
    Upon my sister's death.

MAUDLINE

    Death! She is not dead I hope?

TIM

    No: but she means to be, and that's as good,
    And when a thing's done, 'tis done –
    You taught me that, mother.   15

YELLOWHAMMER

    What is your tutor doing?

TIM

    Making one too, in principal pure Latin,
    Culled out of Ovid *de Tristibus*.

YELLOWHAMMER

    How does your sister look, is she not changed?

TIM

    Changed? Gold into white money was never so changed,   20
    As is my sister's colour into paleness.

Enter MOLL

YELLOWHAMMER

    O here she's brought, see how she looks like death.

TIM

    Looks she like death, and ne'er a word made yet?
    I must go beat my brains against a bed post,
    And get before my tutor.   [*Exit*]

YELLOWHAMMER   Speak, how dost thou?   25

MOLL

    I hope I shall be well, for I am as sick at heart
    As I can be.

YELLOWHAMMER 'Las my poor girl,

    The doctor's making a most sovereign drink for thee,

14 *when a thing's done* Proverbial, with an allusion to a game called 'A thing done'
    cf. Jonson's *Cynthia's Revels* IV.3.160–70, where the context is bawdy.

17 *principal* excellent

18 Ovid's *Tristia* (melancholy poems) was a commonly used Latin text book.

20 *white money* silver

25 *get* beget [a poem]
    thou Yellowhammer and Maudline, all solicitous, now use the affectionate
    'thou' for their daughter.

29 *ingredients* (ingredience Q)

The worst ingredients, dissolved pearl and amber;
We spare no cost girl.
MOLL   Your love comes too late,   30
Yet timely thanks reward it. What is comfort,
When the poor patient's heart is past relief?
It is no doctor's art can cure my grief.
YELLOWHAMMER
All is cast away then;
Prithee look upon me cheerfully.   35
MAUDLINE
Sing but a strain or two, thou wilt not think
How 'twill revive thy spirits: strive with thy fit,
Prithee sweet Moll.
MOLL
You shall have my good will, mother.
MAUDLINE
Why, well said, wench.   40
[MOLL sings]

The Song

Weep eyes, break heart,
My love and I must part;
Cruel fates true love do soonest sever,
O I shall see thee, never, never, never.
O happy is the maid whose life takes end,   45
Ere it knows parent's frown, or loss of friend.
Weep eyes, break heart,
My love and I must part.

Enter TOUCHWOOD SENIOR *with a letter*

MAUDLINE
O, I could die with music: well sung girl!
MOLL
If you call it so, it was.   50
YELLOWHAMMER
She plays the swan, and sings herself to death.
TOUCHWOOD SENIOR
By your leave sir.

pearl and amber were believed to have great medicinal properties; Robert Boyle
says that the 'reducing of pearls to a fine powder affords a rich medicine' (*Works*
(1772) p. 133), and a solution of amber with spirit of wine is 'a friend to the
stomach, the entrails, the nervous parts, and even the head' (p. 329).
37 *strive . . . fit* (a) struggle with your condition, which betokens death (b) put up a
    fight by singing a strain
51 *swan* Swans were proverbially believed to sing only before they died; cf. Orlando
    Gibbons' madrigal, 'The Silver Swan'.

YELLOWHAMMER
   What are you sir? Or what's your business pray?
TOUCHWOOD SENIOR
   I may be now admitted, though the brother
   Of him your hate pursued, it spreads no further;   55
   Your malice sets in death, does it not sir?
YELLOWHAMMER
   In death?
TOUCHWOOD SENIOR   He's dead: 'twas a dear love to him,
   It cost him but his life, that was all sir:
   He paid enough, poor gentleman, for his love.
YELLOWHAMMER
   [Aside] There's all our ill removed, if she were well now.   60
   Impute not, sir, his end to any hate
   That sprung from us; he had a fair wound brought that.
TOUCHWOOD SENIOR
   That helped him forward, I must needs confess:
   But the restraint of love, and your unkindness,
   Those were the wounds that from his heart drew blood;   65
   But being past help, let words forget it too:
   Scarcely three minutes ere his eyelids closed
   And took eternal leave of this world's light,
   He wrote this letter, which by oath he bound me,
   To give to her own hands; that's all my business.   70
YELLOWHAMMER
   You may perform it then, there she sits.
TOUCHWOOD SENIOR
   O with a following look.
YELLOWHAMMER
   Ay, trust me sir, I think she'll follow him quickly.
TOUCHWOOD SENIOR
   Here's some gold
   He willed me to distribute faithfully amongst your servants.   75
YELLOWHAMMER
   'Las what doth he mean sir?
TOUCHWOOD SENIOR
   How cheer you mistress?
MOLL
   I must learn of you sir.
TOUCHWOOD SENIOR
   Here's a letter from a friend of yours,
   And where that fails, in satisfaction   80
   I have a sad tongue ready to supply.

---

56 *sets* declines, wanes
72 *following* as though she were about to follow Touchwood Junior in death

MOLL
  How does he, ere I look on't?
TOUCHWOOD SENIOR
  Seldom better, h'as a contented health now.
MOLL
  I am most glad on't.
MAUDLINE
  Dead sir?   85
YELLOWHAMMER
  He is. Now wife let's but get the girl
  Upon her legs again, and to church roundly with her.
MOLL
  O sick to death he tells me:
  How does he after this?
TOUCHWOOD SENIOR
  Faith, feels no pain at all, he's dead sweet mistress. 90
MOLL
  Peace close mine eyes.   [Swoons]
YELLOWHAMMER
  The girl, look to the girl, wife.
MAUDLINE
  Moll, daughter, sweet girl speak;
  Look but once up, thou shalt have all the wishes of thy heart
  That wealth can purchase.   95
YELLOWHAMMER
  O she's gone for ever, that letter broke her heart.
TOUCHWOOD SENIOR
  As good now, then, as let her lie in torment,
  And then break it.

                    Enter SUSAN

MAUDLINE
  O Susan, she thou lovedst so dear is gone.
SUSAN
  O sweet maid!   100
TOUCHWOOD SENIOR
  This is she that helped her still,
  I've a reward here for thee.
YELLOWHAMMER
  Take her in,
  Remove her from our sight, our shame, and sorrow.
TOUCHWOOD SENIOR
  Stay, let me help thee, 'tis the last cold kindness 105

87 *roundly* smartly, without delay
96 *heart* See note to I.ii.55–6.

I can perform for my sweet brother's sake.

> [*Exeunt* TOUCHWOOD SENIOR *and* SUSAN,
> *carrying* MOLL]

YELLOWHAMMER
All the whole street will hate us, and the world
Point me out cruel: it is our best course wife,
After we have given order for the funeral,
To absent ourselves, till she be laid in ground.   110

MAUDLINE
Where shall we spend that time?

YELLOWHAMMER
I'll tell thee where wench, go to some private church,
And marry Tim to the rich Brecknock gentlewoman.

MAUDLINE
Mass, a match!
We'll not lose all at once, somewhat we'll catch.   115

> *Exit* [*with* YELLOWHAMMER]

[Act V, Scene iii]

Enter SIR OLIVER *and* SERVANTS

SIR OLIVER
Ho, my wife's quickened, I am a man for ever!
I think I have bestirred my stumps i'faith:
Run, get your fellows all together instantly,
Then to the parish church, and ring the bells.

I SERVANT
It shall be done sir.   [*Exit*]   5

SIR OLIVER
Upon my love I charge you villain, that you make a bonfire
before the door at night.

2 SERVANT
A bonfire sir?

SIR OLIVER
A thwacking one I charge you.

---

112 *private* secret
114 *a match* (a) agreed (b) a marriage

2 *bestirred my stumps* been (a) busy (b) sexually active
4, 6 *bells, bonfire* Church bells were rung and bonfires lit to announce important
happenings.

2 SERVANT
[*Aside*] This is monstrous.   [*Exit*]   10

SIR OLIVER
Run, tell a hundred pound out for the gentleman
That gave my wife the drink, the first thing you do.

3 SERVANT
A hundred pounds sir?

SIR OLIVER
A bargain, as our joys grows,
We must remember still from whence it flows,   15
Or else we prove ungrateful multipliers:
The child is coming, and the land comes after;
The news of this will make a poor Sir Walter.
I have struck it home i'faith.

3 SERVANT
That you have, marry, sir.   20
But will not your worship go to the funeral
Of both these lovers?

SIR OLIVER
Both, go both together?

3 SERVANT
Ay sir, the gentleman's brother will have it so,
'Twill be the pitifullest sight; there's such running,   25
Such rumours, and such throngs, a pair of lovers
Had never more spectators, more men's pities,
Or women's wet eyes.

SIR OLIVER
My wife helps the number then?

3 SERVANT
There's such a drawing out of handkerchers,   30
And those that have no handkerchers, lift up aprons.

SIR OLIVER
Her parents may have joyful hearts at this,
I would not have my cruelty so talked on,
To any child of mine, for a monopoly.

3 SERVANT
I believe you sir.   35
'Tis cast so too, that both their coffins meet,
Which will be lamentable.

---

19 *struck it home* hit the target in (a) sport (b) sex
29 *helps the number* adds to the number of mourners
34 *monopoly* (a) both Queen Elizabeth and King James were notorious for granting
   exclusive commercial rights in commodity dealing (b) ironic reference to Sir
   Oliver's having unawares surrendered his marital 'monopoly'
36 *cast* arranged

SIR OLIVER
  Come, we'll see't.

                                                    Ex[eunt]

[Act V, Scene iv]

Recorders dolefully playing. Enter at one door the
coffin of the gentleman, solemnly decked, his sword
upon it, attended by many in black, his brother being
the chief mourner. At the other door, the coffin of the
virgin, with a garland of flowers, with epitaphs pinned
on it, attended by maids and women. Then set them
down one right over against the other, while all the
company seem to weep and mourn; there is a sad song
in the music room.
  [*The company includes* SIR OLIVER *and* LADY KIX, MR
       and MRS ALLWIT, SUSAN *and a* PARSON]

TOUCHWOOD SENIOR
  Never could death boast of a richer prize
  From the first parent, let the world bring forth
  A pair of truer hearts; to speak but truth
  Of this departed gentleman, in a brother,
  Might by hard censure be called flattery,   5
  Which makes me rather silent in his right
  Than so to be delivered to the thoughts
  Of any envious hearer starved in virtue,
  And therefore pining to hear others thrive.
  But for this maid, whom envy cannot hurt   10
  With all her poisons, having left to ages
  The true, chaste monument of her living name,
  Which no time can deface, I say of her
  The full truth freely, without fear of censure;
  What nature could there shine, that might redeem   15

---

0 s.d. *Recorders* were the most common wind instruments of the time, and fre-
  quently mentioned in plays (e.g., *Hamlet* III.ii.367–96). The stage direction here
  corroborates the evidence of the de Witt sketch that the Swan had two doors; the
  music room mentioned here may be the gallery above the stage shown in the
  drawing. The pantomime is discussed in D. Mehl, *The Elizabethan Dumb Show*
  (1965), pp. 148–9.

2 *From the first parent* Since the time of Adam

15–16 *redeem . . . woman* returning to women the perfection that Eve lost through
  the Fall

Perfection home to woman, but in her
Was fully glorious; beauty set in goodness
Speaks what she was, that jewel so infixed;
There was no want of any thing of life,
To make these virtuous precedents man and wife.   20

ALLWIT
Great pity of their deaths.

ALL   Ne'er more pity.

LADY KIX
It makes a hundred weeping eyes, sweet gossip.

TOUCHWOOD SENIOR
I cannot think, there's any one amongst you,
In this full fair assembly, maid, man, or wife,
Whose heart would not have sprung with joy and gladness   25
To have seen their marriage day?

ALL
It would have made a thousand joyful hearts.

TOUCHWOOD SENIOR
Up then apace, and take your fortunes,
Make these joyful hearts, here's none but friends.

[MOLL *and* TOUCHWOOD JUNIOR *rise from their coffins*]

ALL
Alive sir? O sweet dear couple.   30

TOUCHWOOD SENIOR
Nay, do not hinder 'em now, stand from about 'em;
If she be caught again, and have this time,
I'll ne'er plot further for 'em, nor this honest chambermaid
That helped all at a push.

TOUCHWOOD JUNIOR
Good sir, apace.   35

PARSON
Hands join now, but hearts for ever,
Which no parent's mood shall sever.
You shall forsake all widows, wives, and maids:
You, lords, knights, gentlemen, and men of trades:
And if in haste, any article misses,   40

---

16 *but* only
20 *precedents* examples worthy to be followed
34 *at a push* in an emergency
35 s.p. TOUCHWOOD JUNIOR ed. (TOUCHWOOD SENIOR Q)
36 The parson takes up his doggerel wedding service where he left off at III.i.18,
   overlapping half a line.
37 *mood* specifically, anger
40 *article* part of the ceremony; legal term, as is *interline*

Go interline it with a brace of kisses.

TOUCHWOOD SENIOR
Here's a thing trolled nimbly. Give you joy brother,
Were't not better thou should'st have her,
Than the maid should die?

MISTRESS ALLWIT
To you sweet mistress bride.   45

ALL
Joy, joy to you both.

TOUCHWOOD SENIOR
Here be your wedding sheets you brought along with you;
you may both go to bed when you please to.

TOUCHWOOD JUNIOR
My joy wants utterance.

TOUCHWOOD SENIOR
Utter all at night then brother.   50

MOLL
I am silent with delight.

TOUCHWOOD SENIOR
Sister, delight will silence any woman,
But you'll find your tongue again, among maidservants,
Now you keep house, sister.

ALL
Never was hour so filled with joy and wonder.   55

TOUCHWOOD SENIOR
To tell you the full story of this chambermaid,
And of her kindness in this business to us,
'Twould ask an hour's discourse. In brief 'twas she
That wrought it to this purpose cunningly.

ALL
We shall all love her for't.   60

Enter YELLOWHAMMER *and his* WIFE

ALLWIT
See who comes here now.

TOUCHWOOD SENIOR
A storm, a storm, but we are sheltered for it.

YELLOWHAMMER
I will prevent you all, and mock you thus,
You, and your expectations; I stand happy,

---

41 *brace* pair, and also a clasp or support
42 *trolled nimbly* spoken quickly
47 *wedding sheets* the shrouds
50 *Utter* (a) Say (b) Ejaculate
63 *prevent* get in before

Both in your lives, and your hearts' combination.   65
TOUCHWOOD SENIOR
Here's a strange day again.
YELLOWHAMMER   The knight's proved villain,
All's come out now, his niece an arrant baggage;
My poor boy Tim is cast away this morning,
Even before breakfast: married a whore
Next to his heart.
ALL   A whore?
YELLOWHAMMER   His niece forsooth.   70
ALLWIT
I think we rid our hands in good time of him.
MISTRESS ALLWIT
I knew he was past the best, when I gave him over.
What is become of him pray sir?
YELLOWHAMMER
Who, the knight? He lies i'th' knight's ward now.
[To LADY KIX] Your belly, lady, begins to blossom, there's
    no peace for him,   75
His creditors are so greedy.
SIR OLIVER
Master Touchwood, hear'st thou this news?
I am so endeared to thee for my wife's fruitfulness,
That I charge you both, your wife and thee,
To live no more asunder for the world's frowns;   80
I have purse, and bed, and board for you:
Be not afraid to go to your business roundly,
Get children, and I'll keep them.
TOUCHWOOD SENIOR   Say you so sir?
SIR OLIVER
Prove me, with three at a birth, and thou dar'st now.
TOUCHWOOD SENIOR
Take heed how you dare a man, while you live sir,   85
That has good skill at his weapon.

              Enter TIM *and* WELSH GENTLEWOMAN

SIR OLIVER
Foot, I dare you sir.

---

70 *Next to his heart* (a) Nearest in affection (b) On an empty stomach
74 *knight's ward* There were four grades of accommodation in the two Counters
    (debtors' prisons), and the Fleet Prison: the master's side, the knight's ward, the
    twopenny ward and the hole, for those who could pay nothing; cf. Chapman,
    Jonson and Marston, *Eastward Ho!* V.ii.42.
77, 79 *thou, thee* show affectionate respect
82 *roundly* with gusto, but with a pun on 'round' = pregnant

YELLOWHAMMER
Look gentlemen, if ever you saw the picture
Of the unfortunate marriage, yonder 'tis.
WELSH GENTLEWOMAN
Nay, good sweet Tim.   90
TIM
Come from the university,
To marry a whore in London, with my tutor too?
O *tempora*! O *mors*!
TUTOR
Prithee Tim be patient.
TIM
I bought a jade at Cambridge,   95
I'll let her out to execution tutor,
For eighteen pence a day, or Brainford horse races;
She'll serve to carry seven miles out of town well.
Where be these mountains? I was promised mountains,
But there's such a mist, I can see none of 'em.   100
What are become of those two thousand runts?
Let's have a bout with them in the meantime.
A vengeance runt thee!
MAUDLINE   Good sweet Tim, have patience.
TIM
Flectere si nequeo superos Acheronta movebo, mother.
MAUDLINE
I think you have married her in logic Tim.   105
You told me once, by logic you would prove
A whore an honest woman; prove her so Tim
And take her for thy labour.
TIM   Troth I thank you.
I grant you I may prove another man's wife so,
But not mine own.   110

---

88 *saw* ed. (say Q, obsolete past tense of 'see')
93 'O time! O death!' Tim's version of 'O *tempora*! O *mores*' 'Oh, the times! Oh,
    the manners!' (Cicero, *In Catilinam* I.i.I).
95 *jade* (a) worn-out horse (b) whore
96 *execution* performance, in this case, sexual. Tim is saying that as he already has
    a horse in Cambridge, he'll hire out his wife as a prostitute.
97 *Brainford* Brentford (see note II.ii.214); horseracing was one of the entertain-
    ments for visitors; Tim's speech is *double entendre*.
102 *have a bout* have an argument (Q about)
103 *runt* reprove, admonish (though the meaning is stronger here)
104 'Since I cannot prevail upon the powers above, I shall work on the lower regions'
    (Virgil, *Aeneid*, VII, 312).
108 *for thy labour* (a) hard work in argument (b) for your sexual efforts

MAUDLINE
   There's no remedy now Tim,
   You must prove her so as well as you may.

TIM
   Why then my tutor and I will about her,
   As well as we can.
   Uxor non est meretrix, ergo falacis.   115

WELSH GENTLEWOMAN
   Sir if your logic cannot prove me honest,
   There's a thing called marriage, and that makes me honest.

MAUDLINE
   O there's a trick beyond your logic Tim.

TIM
   I perceive then a woman may be honest according to the
   English print, when she is a whore in the Latin. So much for   120
   marriage and logic. I'll love her for her wit, I'll pick out my
   runts there: and for my mountains, I'll mount upon ——

YELLOWHAMMER
   So fortune seldom deals two marriages
   With one hand, and both lucky. The best is,
   One feast will serve them both: marry, for room   125
   I'll have the dinner kept in Goldsmiths' Hall,
   To which kind gallants, I invite you all.

                                 [Exeunt]

FINIS

---

113 *about* deal with (with a sexual innuendo)
115 'A wife is not a whore, therefore you are wrong'
118 *trick* a common play on the Latin *meretrix* = 'whore' and merry 'trick'
121-2 *I'll love . . . there* (a) I'll love her for her cleverness and get my rewards there
     (b) I'll love her for her sexual organ and work away there for my children
122 *mount upon* —— in the sexual sense; the lacuna is in Q
126 *Goldsmiths' Hall* the hall of the Goldsmiths' Company, in Foster Lane off
     Cheapside, 'a proper house, but not large' (*Survey*, I, 305).

APPENDIX A

Thomas Campion uses the following epigram in the sixth chapter of his *Observations in the Art of English Poesie* (1602) as an illustration of English trochaic verse. (See Introduction, p. xiv.) The text here is modernized from that in *Campion's Works*, ed. Percival Vivian (Oxford, 1909), p. 46.

The Eighth Epigram

Barnzy stiffly vows that he's no cuckold,
Yet the vulgar everywhere salutes him
With strange signs of horns, from every corner;
Wheresoe'er he comes, a sundry 'Cuckoo'
Still frequents his ears; yet he's no cuckold.   5
But this Barnzy knows that his Matilda,
Scorning him, with Harvy plays the wanton.
Knows it? Nay desires it, and by prayers
Daily begs of heav'n that it for ever
May stand firm for him; yet he's no cuckold.   10
And 'tis true, for Harvy keeps Matilda,
Fosters Barnzy, and relieves his household,
Buys the cradle, and begets the children,
Pays the nurses, every charge defraying,
And thus truly plays Matilda's husband: 15
So that Barnzy now becomes a cipher,
And himself th'adulterer of Matilda.
Mock not him with horns, the case is altered;
Harvy bears the wrong, he proves the cuckold.

Walter R. Davis suggests that this epigram may allude to the writers Barnabe Barnes and Gabriel Harvey. Campion also mocked Barnes in his first book of Latin epigrams (published in 1619 though written at various times), of which the 17th, 'In Barnum', ridicules Barnes; coincidentally, Epigram 143 describes another complaisant cuckold, Crispinus. (See *The Works of Thomas Campion*, ed. Walter R. Davis (New York, 1969), pp. 305, 410, 417.)

A similar theme, but with added commercial, misogynist and sectarian implications, is found in a Jacobean ballad in the Harleian MS. (3910, fols. 41ᵛ–42). The text here is modernized from the version in *Old English Ballads 1553–1625*, ed. Hyder E. Rollins (Cambridge, 1920), pp. 196–97.

1

Who would not be a cuckold,
To have a handsome wife?
Who would not be a wittol,
To lead a merry life?
  Though many do disdain it,
  And scorn to have the name,
  Yet others entertain it,
  And never blush for shame.

2

The good-wife, like a peacock,
She jets in brave attire;
The good-man, like a meacock,*
Sits smoking o'er the fire:
  He never dares reprove her,
  But lets her have her will;
  Nor cares how many loves her,
  So she the purse do fill.

3

Some men attain to maces,
Through bounty of their dames,
And cover all disgraces,
If well they play their games.
  But when the sole commanding
  Amongst the females fall,
  For want of understanding
  They commonly mar all.

4

Nor doth alone the city
Such precedents afford:
In court, the more the pity,
Some ladies play the lord:
  And then to be in fashion,
  She turns Catholical –
  O vile abomination,
  The Pope can pardon all!

5

Are women thus devoted
To levities by kind?
Or are the men so doted
To see and yet be blind?
  But profit and promotion
  The world do over-rule
  And counterfeit devotion
  Can make the wise a fool.

---

* *meacock* an effeminate and cowardly man